On Afterlife

You Will Get There from Here

G. V. Loewen

Strategic Book Publishing and Rights Co.

Copyright 2012
All rights reserved — G. V. Loewen

No part of this book may be reproduced or transmitted in any form or by any means, graphic, electronic, or mechanical, including photocopying, recording, taping, or by any information storage retrieval system, without the permission, in writing, from the publisher.

Strategic Book Publishing and Rights Co.
12620 FM 1960, Suite A4-507
Houston, TX 77065
www.sbpra.com

ISBN: 978-1-61897-114-2

Typography and page composition by J. K. Eckert & Company, Inc.

For M.C.B.,
whose absence is still oddly present,
and whose presence has taken the form
of an afterlife.

Contents

Chapter 1—The Nature of Mortal Memory 1
Recalling the Calling of the Work of Life

Chapter 2—Types of Belief Regarding the Afterlife..........29
Part 1: Unevaluated Return

Chapter 3—Types of Belief Regarding the Afterlife..........49
Part 2: Evaluated Return

Chapter 4—Types of Belief Regarding the Afterlife..........65
Part 3: Evaluated Continuity

Chapter 5—Types of Belief Regarding the Afterlife..........81
Part 4: Unevaluated Continuity

Chapter 6—Everything as Not Anything—Nothingness 101

Chapter 7—On Living on after Living....................123
Preparing for an Afterlife

Epilogue: The Death of Death 149
A Few Words on Indefinite Life

Cited and Suggested Readings............................155

1

The Nature of Mortal Memory

Recalling the Calling of the Work of Life

We are all well aware of the presence of death in life. Indeed, we are so aware of it that we have developed a duplicitous relationship with it. On one hand, there is the knowledge that we ourselves will eventually depart this earth. We do not know exactly when this will occur but we know it is inevitable. Depending upon our changing circumstances, we may await this moment with dread or resignation, anxiety, or even optimism. Our understanding of our own demise is ambiguous because we cannot link up its actual timing with the fact of its future occurrence. We become serially aware of death through the passages of others who leave this life before us; they may do so in ways so familiar to us that we imagine that we, too, may "go like them someday." In fact, our understanding of our own deaths may be said to come from the deaths of others, as it is one of the paradoxes of human existence that we cannot experience our own death per se. Watching people die, intimately or from afar, affects us as no other event can. One is forced to admit to one's own mortality as one accepts the mortality of others.

Apart from a few extremes—the criminal sadism of certain members of the Gestapo or some murderers, for example—human beings almost universally mourn the death of another, and take no pleasure in it. Relief, possibly, as when a loved one finally succumbs to a lengthy terminal illness, but not pleasure. Even here, relief may be accompanied by a bad conscience, or even guilt. Just as we are not supposed to "speak ill of the dead"—once again, with certain exceptions—we are also not supposed to partake in anything but the shadows of existence and mournful memory when confronted by human finitude. One hopes one does not "get used" to death in any familiar manner, and one of the major traumas of combat is that veterans must adapt to the normative moral conscience of civil and more or less peaceable society that they were trained to ignore in order to function during the crisis of wartime.

We are insulated from a too-personal awareness of death. We experience it vicariously, through the deaths of others, and also by analogy, in that their deaths might be kindred to our own. Yet this dual relationship with death in life manifests itself in a much more complex order of belief and custom that has taken shape from the earliest origins of human ancestry and has inspired some of the most profound reflections on the nature of what we are. It is the structure and diversity of these reflections that will be the subject of this book.

The confluence of death in life creates the idea of the afterlife, because this idea also describes what occurs after death. After-life is also after-death. Life may be exciting, tolerable, inhumane, or grotesque, but most of us have the almost innate sense that we can "get through it" if there is some other version of it laying ahead that will either balance the books of this life or change us so that we no longer have any mortal concerns, whatever might have happened to us before the transformation took place. In this way, we are able to negotiate both the day-to-day travails of living on, the "slings and arrows of outrageous fortune," or even "the petty insolence of officials," to remind us of two apt descriptions of the happenstance and the quotidian respectively found in Hamlet's soliloquy on existence, but as well attempt to comprehend our own situation with regard to death. The dual relationship we have with our experience with death, both our knowledge and our ignorance of it, creates a duet of understanding.

We generally know as a fact that the dead do not return, and yet we also fear their imagined or possible return. This tension is played out in dark or edgy humor which is at once frightening and then suddenly relieving; in desperate struggles of the imagination where we might lie awake at night and debate whether we have led "a good life" or not; or by cathartic battles against the "undead," as in a genre of popular video games.

Here is a typical example of the first of these scenarios: it is standard practice during the training of new police officers that a visit to the morgue is obligatory, with all its attendant processes and protocols. After first emptying a fellow officer's revolver of its cartridges, a group of policemen escorted their new colleague to see the coroner.

As is often the case in a larger city, there were a few corpses lying out on the trestles, either presently being examined or pending. While standing beside one of them, the rookie was suddenly gripped firmly by the wrist by a hand that felt as cold as a block of marble. The hapless officer screamed, and everyone else began to laugh uproariously, including the coroner. Another police colleague had, of course, posed as one of the dead after first resting his hand and forearm in a bag of ice. No doubt such pranks are also standard practice in initiation rituals of all kinds, perhaps especially in masculine-dominated domains where the irresponsible phrase "boys will be boys" still has some relevance. The humor this kind of mischief entails straddles that odd threshold between what we know to be true and what we nonetheless fear is not always, or not quite, true. Not unlike those with well diagnosed "phobias"—the fear of elevators is a classic one in this regard, where we are aware of the lengthy odds against anything untoward occurring to us while we are occupants of one, but nevertheless shy away and ascend by the stairs—the sensibility that establishes a tension between so-called rational and irrational thinking animates much of our daily life.

The context where such a tension is most sharply brought to light is the one that presents the confluence of death with life. Of course, corpses do not reach out for us from beyond the grave. And yet we are somehow not entirely surprised if, against all experience and rational thought, something bizarre or eldritch suddenly occurs, rending our day-to-day consciousness with a radical ferocity. Although we might be quite shocked and frightened out of our wits by such an event, it is this very fright that belies our underlying expectations of both the living and the dead. For the dead were once alive, and walked the earth with us as we ourselves walk. We too will "join" them—if such a word can have any real meaning here—and the mystery of just exactly where the life of the living went to is brought into the fullest glare of day. Shock and fear are the first things we feel not because we think that this is something that in fact cannot happen—quite the opposite. If we had only a rational attitude towards death then even the seemingly intentional movement of a cadaver would not frighten us so much as make us curious, skeptical, and most of all, suspicious of the very kind of prank that was played on the unfortunate officer.

Under ideally rational conditions, the rookie would have gripped the corpse back or used his other hand to disengage it while uncovering the body sheet and investigating such a phenomenon, whatever its cause. That such a reaction would be extremely unusual no matter what culture we hail from, is testament to the point that we already have expectations of the dead which include the belief—an amalgam of ultimate human aspiration and anxiety—that the dead are still alive. If they are not exactly with us, then they are also not exactly without us either.

Death could not be a subject of either fear or humor, nor further the mischievous combination of the two of them, if we did not sustain this existential tension within ourselves. The inevitability of dying and then "being" dead—again, we are not sure what real meaning such a phrase could have in this regard—is conjured in quips such as "death and taxes." Though we also know that there are some people who do not pay taxes, most of us feel that taxation is the experience most like death. Yet it is more historically accurate to compare death to other seemingly universal rites of passage that occur to all human beings no matter one's origin or creed.

Birth, puberty, "marriage" or some such socially sanctioned union—meant traditionally for the purposes of reproduction and kinship alliance, and more recently for the arrangement of the inheritance of property—and, perhaps, dying itself, are the hallmarks of the human life cycle. To participate in all of them, and in their expected order, is to participate in the nature of humanity and has been likened to being part of the order of nature itself. The step between the idea that states, "This is simply the ways things are," and the idea that "this is the way things are supposed to be" is a short one. Our cultural imaginations are severely limited by what we are born into, and this is precisely the point. Societies could not reproduce themselves with any efficacy unless their respective children were trained and taught only in the ways of this or that culture, and in no other.

Children who grow up in families with mixed cultural ancestries face a unique challenge. They must at once be attuned to more than one cultural system, and this entails an ability to shift one's loyalties at a moment's notice between beliefs and customs that may very well conflict. It is commonplace to hear persons speak of this kind of scenario when the two parents are involved in a cross-cultural relationship. But we should bear in mind that such relationships are not restricted to different ethnicities, nationalities, or even races. In fact, marriage across social class is often seen as the most difficult dialectic, with religion also constituting a serious challenge to intimacy. Aside from the obvious logistical limitations—rich and poor seldom meet in intimate settings in our society—as well as the outright bigotries the classes have against one another, it is no surprise that these conjugations are the most rare by far of all known kinds of marriage. Remarks at weddings are usually limited to how different the mates are to one another in terms of their personalities—she is an extrovert and he is an introvert, that kind of thing. But personalities themselves have their sources in wider social structures. Moreover, the "styles" of parenting children undergo—authoritarian and laissez-faire are often compared here—also can be located within the ambit of the kinds of ethnic, class, education, work, and immigration backgrounds the parents have themselves lived through. There are statistics for every sort of marriage regarding numbers of children, parenting style, whether or not one or two parents work, or neither, divorce rates, suicide, adultery, etc. It is well known that the global average divorce rate in North America is about fifty percent. Half of all marriages end "prematurely," that is, before the death of one or the other spouses. One of the reasons sociological commentaries are not generally welcome at weddings is not that we wish to remain, at least for that day, blissfully ignorant of the wider social realities that impinge upon our attempts at intimacy—in much the same way that we may ignore the presence of death during our living hours of activity and love—but rather that we are in fact very much aware of how fragile our social relations are.

Akin to the character in Edgar Allen Poe's "Premature Burial," where a kind of paranoia has gripped us so firmly that we forget the living context of our contemporary reality and imagine that we have been committed to the ground whilst still alive, we are bidden to try not to recall the likely futures of our plans while we enact them. This human ability, bequeathed to us in myth by the Greek demigod Prometheus who hid from human beings the hour of their respective deaths, enables all projects to carry on with the "as if" quality that they can, in fact, be completed as imagined. This ability to cognitively separate specific action directed at finite goals from the absolute value of human finiteness—that is, we live on as if we are not mortal after all—makes us different from all other life as we know it. No wonder the Greek gods punished Prometheus in horrible ways, because his gift allowed to us to be as the gods already were; to imagine that we were immortal and thus our works and lives could take on a real meaning that endured through unending generations. We are in a somewhat unique position regarding this gift today, of course, as we universally face, or don't face, our own extinction.

So the rites of passage have built into them a basic optimism. In spite of the risks of infant mortality or other genetic markers for childhood disease, and in spite of the travails new parents imagine that they will undergo in raising their children, births are almost universally celebrated. In spite of the dangers of adolescence and the real threat of the loss of their children's loyalties to other social institutions and their peer group, puberty is a harbinger of ultimate autonomy and adulthood, and thus acknowledged as a future-looking stage even while many parents mourn the loss of childhood "innocence." Marriage is always greeted with great fanfare and joy in spite of the rates of divorce; spousal and child abuse; the internal alienation and loneliness both partners may feel if work prevents them from spending enough time together; and conflicts over the raising of children, styles and frequency of sexual intimacies, and money. Indeed, while the overall divorce rate is well known, it is less known that the percentages rise sharply the younger the two spouses are, with rates approaching eighty-five percent if those who wed are younger than twenty-five. While it is likely that older persons settle down with the awareness that it might be "now or never," it is also clear that younger people simply change, often drastically, during their twenties and thirties, and it should come as no surprise that in our own time period, with more equality of income opportunities, that persons feel that they should not have to be stuck with someone they cannot love or cherish due to "personal" differences. The blanket legal clause, "irreconcilable differences," is meant to cover all of the possible variations on this theme, without regard to their social sources. Without children, this parting of ways is generally a short-term transition. At the same time, it is also well known that children are better off the less conflict between parents is extant. Divorce, too, is emblazoned with the vision of a future.

It is only in death, most especially if the burial is premature, that we are reminded that the solace of the future has a definite limit. Yet throughout all of humanity's written history, there have been strong concepts of the afterlife that promise an extension of what we normally feel while alive. If each of the universal rites of passage is forward-looking, a better future might well await us after we have passed through each rite. This is surely the case in our imaginations, notwithstanding the statistical evidence, regarding marriage. Further, we know that most children grow up to become more or less functioning adults, even if they have suffered in the ways only children can. There is a paradox involved in our confrontation with death, however, that allows us to acknowledge the difficulties of living as a way to assuage the grief of immanent loss. While suffering is underplayed with regard to the other three rites, with death it may be overplayed, as in the idea of the "merciful release," or "eternal rest"—the sense of ultimate and infinite peace and the communion with another world that is beyond both human torpor and concern. We know we cannot control the character of our future looking which attempts to reach beyond death, and so we let a basic optimism prevail in our acceptance that this final rite of passage hides from us its true nature. That death is hardly the only mystery in human life allows us to reflect on the kinds of happenstances we can to a certain extent control. Desire is also clad in mysterious garments, violence in an armor that protects its passionate secrets, and ecstasy and joy allow us only their feelings but not their intellect. Human life as whole cloth, and the circumference of its cycle as a completed journey, leaves much to the imagination.

The chief way in which we negotiate the gaps in our knowledge concerning our own lives and the lives of others is through the memory of experiences we have had together. Memory is at once an intensely personal folder of unshared experiences as well as being an archive of events and perhaps even feelings that we deem to have been shared, intimately or otherwise. It is private, because we can never know with certainty that we have truly shared anything with anyone else, in the sense that our feelings and our beings are unique to this world. Language is the universal medium of the exchange of interpretations, and not identities. No experience affects the more than one in the same way that it affects the one.

With each of us keeping these memories to ourselves while at the same time trying to share them through various kinds of language as best we can, once again human consciousness presents itself as a double life. The publicity we give to our thoughts and feelings is often quite guarded. We are aware of how others might interpret what we say and do. We surround ourselves with others whom we can trust to give us the benefit of the doubt. If we have any real enemies in this life—aside from ourselves in our less alert moments—it is those who seek to gain insight into our way of life and use it against us, exploiting the weaknesses or foibles of character that we all exhibit from time to time. In doing so, they serve us as ironic reminders not of the presence of memory but of its lapses. It is common for someone to express regret that he or she did not recall the true nature of this or that person. Our friends gently remind us that "he or she is just like that," which is enough for us to recall what "like that" really means. We make a note to be more careful in the future, and not merely with a specific person, which may have been the subject of the current faux pas, but of all persons "like that" and their would-be allies. Memory is thus linked to anticipation in a myriad of small moments and motifs. The past and the future cannot do without one another.

Even though memory gives the appearance of being solely concerned with what has gone before, it is actually more oriented to the future than we would guess simply because memory itself is selective, convenient, and not only socially and historically constructed, but politically and ethically constructed as well. Nietzsche skillfully reminds us of the relationship between actual events and our vanities when he states, "Memory says I have done this. Pride says I cannot have done this. At last, memory yields." We rewrite our own pasts just as nation-states or other large social institutions are apt to rewrite their histories, especially given that all pasts—personal, national, and global—contain the darker presence of an ambiguous human consciousness. Whatever the present convenience may be, our memory is tractable to it. If we wish to "turn over a new leaf," or put into practice some new year's resolutions, we must overcome the inertia of what we have been like before. Indeed, "changing oneself" requires that others around us also change. We cannot see ourselves differently in the same light of those who refuse to acknowledge that any change, personal or social, has occurred. We may well be convinced that we are merely deluding ourselves if those in whom we put the confidence of confidences and the trust of trusts do not at least play along. Of course, on a broader scale, it is just this kind of "bandwagon" approach to political and social movements that breathes life into ideas that could be disastrously unethical, as in the chicanery that saw "the Jews" as a threat to European culture and art. Without even approaching the massive violence inherent in such ideas, our appeal to close friends to let us become something different may occasion the loss of the previous community and the building of a new one, not unlike the process by which a key witness may be given a new identity and the means to start a new life elsewhere. If such a strategy fails, the person is tried and convicted as his old self—in legalistic terms, he may be assassinated by criminals for what he had exposed during his "previous life."

Yet we need not even imagine such plots as appear in popular crime and legal television shows to understand the effect of the necessary mutability of memory. If we are to make anything of ourselves at all, we must overcome whatever it is we understand to have been weak or lax in ourselves. "What is holding you back?" is a question regularly put to us by the mirror and by other human beings. The American sociologist Charles Cooley called this phenomenon "the looking-glass self," in that our very identities are socially constructed and perpetuated by those around us. The simple proof of this lies in the need for others to change their opinions and beliefs regarding our persons, or failing that, for other persons with the necessary new viewpoints to appear and take their place. Only when this happens can we be said to have become some other person.

Along with this change, but perhaps unequal to it in its motive force, is the task of rewriting our own mortal memories of what we had been, to allow a more subtle egress from the past self into the new one. If we accomplish this in the manner Nietzsche suggests is commonplace, it will also become all the more convenient to assuage future lapses of character or ethics—or, if one has a correspondingly weak social conscience, perhaps lapses of kindness—and thus the rewriting of memory is revealed as a constant and continuous action upon thought. The archiving of our experiences in our minds cannot but pass through this kind of filter; living cannot be done without such a mechanism. We cannot, first of all, recall every event that has ever happened to us, much less remember every thought that has occurred to us. Nor can we recall what others have told us they have undergone or felt, or their thoughts, or their motives. This seeming infinity of human behavior is automatically filtered before it can even qualify as a memory. And once ensconced as a mindful "memorial," it is subject to yet further transformations. There is quite literally an afterlife of living experience. Memory is itself the afterlife of both action and thought. As such, it provides for us the most intimate and potent metaphor for the death of what was once living. The past is thus the death of the present while at the same time being the augur of the future.

No future can be imagined without access to what has been reconstituted by memory—either personal or official political memories, as we shall see below—and no present becomes recognizable without a momentary and immediate comparison with what we think we know already. Needless to say, not all of this comparing and contrasting is entirely conscious. The social self runs on the rails of expected and normative behavior. It reads the social map with one lazy eye, as it were, and can usually do so with aplomb. The alteration of memory through the motivation of egotism, the suasion of others, the ethics of confidences and trusts, the scheming of other kinds of the both of them—or simply due to our empirically faulty senses—allows both a vision of what can come next as well as who we might become tomorrow.

Yet the manner in which we create memory and modify it is more complex than a simple pride or an instrumental weeding out of the irrelevant. It is also more than a mental operation. The land on which we live is haunted, often mutely, by the echoes of the experiences and deeds of our predecessors, both claimed and rejected, both acknowledged and repressed, and the interplay amongst memories we privately or officially celebrate, pay homage to, or with humility recognize, and all of those forgotten or unforgettable echoes constitute memory as both an act and as a way of thinking. Over many years of research into memorialization, I found that twelve separate ways of creating memories and thence maintaining them were generally available to persons living in our society. These twelve could be grouped into three larger and more abstract categories, which I called "personal narratives," "spaces of memory," and "rewriting histories." Each of these in turn created a landscape of the dead. This landscape performed both the functions of helping us to live with what appears to be radically unlike life, as well as providing the ignorance of history needed to allow the proper official functioning of institutional spaces which represent history as an unchangeable past and therefore done with, and historical persona as dead and therefore without further influence. That is, it is often not enough to simply acknowledge with a casual and "philosophical" nod that death also inhabits the same space as that which does life. We also must come to terms with the fact that how we personally recall events might be quite different from how society prefers to remember them—the deeds of warfare being the most obvious example that causes such a disconnect between real persons who have lived through it and the official histories of the nations and governments who brought war upon themselves and their citizens.

If one experiences the trauma of the death of one just now alive and loved, or the eldritch event of the revisiting by the long dead, or yet the stolid stonework of monuments to anonymous death, the personification of history undertakes the arduous journey of reconciling the fact of death in life, and the fact that life appears to be ultimately the weaker sibling. Therefore, I called the first of the three categories of memorialization "personal narratives." This category has four subforms, which one might characterize as the following: i) the "bad old days," ii) the "good old days," iii) "I can't help the way I am," and iv) "I couldn't help the way I was." Let us explore each of them from both the perspective of their presence as part of a magical landscape of memory, and their recollective power to transform biographical events of both self and others.

The conjuring and reminiscing of the "bad old days" preserves the idea that no matter how difficult the present is, it is still much better than what one had gone through to get to the present. This may most poignantly be reflected in the feeling that the death of a loved one—perhaps one who had been terminally ill and had suffered for years—was more of a relief and release than a tragedy. The tragedy, in fact, had already occurred and was part of the living, or dying, history of the individuals concerned. The German philosopher of interpretation, Hans-Georg Gadamer, suggests, "It seems as if the repression of death, which belongs to life itself, must be made good again by those who remain among the living in a way which is natural for them" (1996:67 [original 1985]). We, in the wake of death, whether it is waking, wakeful, or presented as a celebratory wake, must be again awake to life. Life returns in spite of the fact that it too must end, and it always returns in this manner. Although the periods of both recollection, memorialization, and renunciation vary according to the intimacy of those grief-stricken, one has to "get on with it," and gradually let go the bitterness of accepting all forms of loss. Describing one's own history or cultural history as lesser and more evil than the present is also a common structure in the presentation of history itself, especially since the conflict between the ancients and moderns and the birth of the idea of progress. We have generally internalized and individuated "progress" as an ideal, and when progress can no longer be effected, or further, when there is actual regression as there may be in debilitating illness, we speak of preferring "quality of life" over quantity, and attempt to preserve a covenant with those who will more than likely remain behind to fulfill tasks set by the departed.

Indeed, Gadamer reminds us that it is our recent technology that has prolonged life beyond one's own experience of life. Our empirical inability to experience death is an ancient puzzle, but the obfuscation of the boundary between what was once clearly demarcated leads to an irresponsibility about, and even a denial of, the end. The final moment might be delayed, but the cost of holding at bay what is the natural conclusion for all life as we know it is, in fact, the cost of human dignity. This is the cost of what it means to become fully human, a state of being only consummated, apparently paradoxically, in death.

In our own day, persons have begun to question the medical model of life. The resistance to stem cell research may well be a manifestation of this suspicion. Any model that prefers quantity of life over quality sets itself up for a blanket wariness that withholds its support for other new technologies that could actually increase both. The suspicion rests on experience, and most importantly, on memory—for example, the memories of loved ones forced by law to be kept alive against their will, or to undergo treatments for diseases that prolong also the life of the diseases. It is no surprise that some of us are ill at ease with any medical triumph that promises a better life by changing the previous life in a radical manner. The idea that we are "playing God" may be only a useful rhetoric, a rallying point for persons whose social locations are perennially at the margins of the institutions which seem to decide such things on our behalf, but for the benefit of yet others who do not necessarily bear the emotional responsibility for watching their fellow humans struggle with dying and death. Many persons are not quite ready to make the life they had been living into an afterlife, and yet live on. We will speak in more detail about these issues in the final chapter and epilogue, but suffice to say for now that "the bad old days" might not be as bad as all that. Even if the estrangement from life while one is still living occurs through the imposition of forces maleficent, or even anonymous, any narrative characterized by the "bad old days" aids our individual and collective memories in telling the tale in the first place. Our progress is defined with too much ease. We lived through this or that crisis while others did not. Their sacrifices ring true for it is we who witness the truth of the return of what lives on from its temporary absence or interruption.

A second form of the structure of personal narrative is, of course, the inverse of the first. Here the past is put on a pedestal and the present is deplored. This in itself is an ancient idea, and characterizes Greek mythology and thought far back into written history and its documentation of the Hellenic area. Beginning with the Homeric narratives of the Trojan War, "the good old days" theme animates a kind of rationalization of suffering in the present. What we now must undergo is either what we deserve, given our faded status, or as part of fate itself, a natural order of things that we simply had the bad luck to stumble into. The ancient Hebrew narrative of the expulsion from paradise also demonstrates this thematic structure. The badness of the present, with its "work or die" motif well known to all inhabitants of both agricultural and industrial societies, takes its cue from the sense that humanity itself committed a transgression that excommunicated it from the paradise of the "good old days." The fin de siècle period, beginning around 1880 and encompassing the remainder of the Victorian and Edwardian periods up to the start of the apocalypse of the First World War—including as its attendant harbinger the foundering of the Titanic—held within it a cynicism about mainstream views of progress. This ultimately nihilistic viewpoint is our most recent version of the "good old days" motif. Although the horrific events of the twentieth century support the face validity of the idea that previous periods were somehow much healthier, more moral, safer, harder working, gentle, caring, and personal—to name a few of the usual suspects—than is our own age, empirically we must accept that more people have a better quality of life globally than at any other time since perhaps the beginning of agriculture, and certainly since the industrial revolution swept in our current mode of production. The "good old days" is pre-eminently a form of nostalgia.

Even children perform narrative in this manner when they gradually confront more and more incipient responsibility in their worlds. The phantasmagorical congeries of the world-creating abilities of youngsters are often narrowed and perhaps even destroyed by their forced participation within ever more rationalized institutional life. One look at the difference between the curiosity and imagination of the kindergarten child as opposed to the eighteen-year-old who has just been released from high school should underscore such a view. The enrichment of one's elder's history at the expense of the present can equally be used as a form of social control, and thus could be considered an effort at preserving the attention of individuals on the organization of a civil society. When one's arrogance about one's own age, generation, or future is tempered by the humility that a glorious past confers upon its descendants, the "good old days" narrative is at work. Furthermore, one can look forward in due course, after the "dues of life" have been paid, to one's own version of a history romanticized at the expense of yet further neophytes.

Perhaps most importantly, the "good old days" prepares those who claim to have lived though them and may be given some credit or responsibility for constructing them. Nostalgia of this sort is thus an attempt to assuage the anxiety about the nearing horizon of finitude and the onset of the direct cognizance of one's own death. There may be a powerful link between what, in fact, made the "good old days" good, and our present ability to do what is good for ourselves and others. If we find ourselves in situations where we are at a loss, we come perilously near the abyss of loss itself. If we do not think we know what to do, then we are standing next to that place where one does not know anything at all. This space is that of non-thought, and can only be called by its true name by those who still have the capacity of human consciousness, that is, those who remain alive in the presence of death. What both the "bad old days" and the "good old days" share is the shying away of a time where all histories merge into the darkness of the total loss of memory. The ever-creeping shadows of memory loss certainly haunt all of us, and it is notorious that older persons, if they find they have forgotten some trivial thing, chide themselves in the presence of others for slipping into the beginnings of dementia. We know that one of the prime functions of memory, whatever may be its cultural contents and its wisdoms, is to keep alive the notion that we ourselves are still alive. We know we cannot know the present without the past. Whether the present is judged as superior or inferior is a matter of secondary importance.

The third aspect of the category of "personal narratives" in relation to memorialization offers an exoneration of the present through an extension of present circumstances back in time. "I can't help the way I am" makes a nature out of the happenstance of culture and society. Therefore the present is the past, and the past is continually re-presenced as the present. One is a living vehicle for what also lived in history, and therefore the ability of death to cut this continuity is mitigated. This motif is primarily used to either accept or proselytize a person's or a culture's fables of self, whether mythological or ideological or perhaps even idiosyncratic. If one understands oneself to harbor weaknesses, and is burdened with the stigma of others' viewpoints, the "way one is" becomes a perpetual excuse. If one is intent on dominating others and showing them the error of their ways, then the "way one is" becomes a model for action and an example to be emulated. It remains a perpetual weapon against criticism. Here also the best defense against self-critique is a good offense that criticizes others. We remain what we have been, and what we have been is visibly present in us. "I can't help the way I am" carries with it the elliptical "There is no reason for me to deny this because there is no real reason I should change it." The vaunted presence of that which is empirically unavailable serves in its turn to not merely exonerate the shortcomings of the present as it is, but also to avoid both the "old days" narratives: the "good," which in this case might lead to low societal or individual morale in the present, and the "bad," which would be an actual admission of the weakness of any particular society's history and might suggest yet further reflection upon corresponding current inequities.

So at once we have a sense that what we have been, in fact, is part of our nature and is thus immutable, but also because it is by definition who we are it must also represent the best self, otherwise nature itself would not have become defined by it. The proper relationship to one's history, and the history of one's people, is thus further reinforced by the simple inertia the now "natural" order has. All traditional cultures use the "I can't help the way I am" style of memory as the most convenient manner of reproducing culture in their children, and it is often used either merely naively or with a certain knowing irony. For modern society to use it at all suggests only laziness or torpor.

The final sub-form of the first category of memorialization—that of "personal narratives"—involves a satire of cultural or personal history as often a kind of perverse overcoming. "I can't help the way I was" suggests that at the time, in spite of recent improvements and the vision of hindsight, there was nothing that could have been done, by oneself or anyone, about the events of history. Whether it is water or blood flowing under the proverbial bridge, we must accept it for what it was. Perhaps this is the most realistic of the four forms of this first category, and yet its use of self-satire and self-effacement might be a clue to a kind of suppression of historical truth. Whenever there is trauma, tragedy, or crisis, we are aware that we will be judged by our successors. We will be judged by whatever may constitute the future, and that whatever also may make that future flawed—whether imperfect or, worse, intolerable. We, as those who live in what is now the present, but also as the "to be historical," bear responsibility for these outcomes. How do we share a blame which we know will come but which we at present have the passing luxury to massage? The sense that what we have done might have been done differently is often a potent impetus for the rewriting of history. The accusation that rests in the eyes of our children holds within it all of the vague interdictions of other possibilities, and thus altered outcomes. Each successive generation passes through such a series of action, bad conscience, attempted rationalization, successful exoneration, and finally, abdication. In its melange of anger, denial, and acceptance it is similar to other more famous forms of mourning. It in itself is a process of memorialization that individuals encounter and project upon the landscapes of both their own minds and the world at large. The threshold that marks that cultural memory which lies just beyond mortal memory is impregnable by normative methods. What is gone is gone for both good and for bad. All of our methods for retracing and rehabilitating the past—archaeology, archival research, oral narrative, etc.—are kinds of prosthetic devices in this regard. This is simply because although we are human, the very definition of what it means to be human has shifted. The humanity that our ancestors knew themselves to be a part of is no longer what we are, more or less, and the imposition of what we new humans have constructed for ourselves has undergone radical change even in the past century. We can know at least this both empirically and textually, that is, through direct observation of the world and through reading about other worlds, and the ever-changing landscape of living memory presents perhaps our most critical challenge with regard to ethics and social maturity.

When the last survivor of a crisis dies, whether it was a family mishap, the civil war, or even the Holocaust, what can we know of what is equally obviously still our own? The use of self-satire, which reminds us of the darkly humorous relationship to our own history we often inhabit, is most fully evident in this fourth sub-form. We "cannot help the way we were" simply because we were not there to help. Who we were, as persons or cultures, was not, we imagine, what we are today. The translation of history one observes with the previous three sub-forms of this initial structure of memorialization does not recur in this final form. It cannot do so because the presence of what is not and cannot be present is too forceful to deny.

Yet, despite this force, it is the second category of memorialization, "spaces of memory," that addresses itself to remedying just such a problem of living only in our own age. Once again there are at least four characteristics to this category, and I have called them: v) "the immobility of death," vi) "the rationalization of source," vii) "the replication of the lived," and viii) "the ignoring of source." Of the attempts at shifting the apparently unmovable nature of the first characteristic in the second category, Gadamer informs us that,

> There is perhaps no other experience in human life which so clearly marks the limits placed on that modern control of nature acquired through science and technology. It is precisely these enormous technological advances, with their goal of the artificial preservation of life, which reveal the absolute limit of what we can achieve. The prolongation of life finally becomes a prolongation of death and a fading away of the experience of the self. This process culminates in the gradual disappearance of the experience of death. (1996:62 [1985]).

No doubt we have, especially since the Enlightenment, extended (often prosthetically) the quantity of lived years, as well as the probability that an infant will survive a certain number of years against odds previously much higher. Yet the horizon we seek to push beyond the limits of human experience lies beyond the limits of human knowledge. We will have more to say about the near future of human evolution in the epilogue below, but unless and until we become another species entirely—most likely a genetic and cybernetic hybrid—we will always fall short in this effort. The response to the ultimate denial of mere technological artifice has been most plainly the erecting of monuments to the dead, which are at the same time monuments to death itself.

These monuments, large and small—imposing signposts dotting the horizon yet sometimes just as often underfoot and reminding us to watch our step—often appear to be as immovable as what they metaphorically carry. Their metaphorical weight grounds them in the ground of memory. They are buried in history even as they delineate the action of the past. For instance, national battlefield sites are literally littered with hundreds if not thousands of monuments, giving a blow-by-blow account of the events that transpired in those fatal times and places. Tours are constructed around the flow of the imagined action, and one can follow the movements of troops, artillery, cavalry, ships, etc. by simply reading the signs. These historical highways re-presence all that can be known and said about what is "knowable" about the past in the present. The monumentality of the marking of spaces of death, heroic or tragic, allows for the reproduction of the mentality that indeed death can be either one or the other or both, but never neither, never simply death as the ceasing of organic consciousness and, so far as the living may know, the passage from something to nothing.

Even at the moment of death our memories exert themselves upon the translation between the reality of life and the mere metaphor of its absence. It comes into play in the hospital bed: the stillborn gaze of vacant sockets, the breath arrested in mid-air, and the silent awe of the onlookers. All are now not what once just was. All are "mere" metaphors for a now passed experience of life. What was alive immediately becomes part of an afterlife. Part of us has also died in the hour of another's death, and we must always wait and see what might replace this aspect of our experience and of ourselves. Will a new member of the family be born and attention and affection be thus transferred to him or her? Will a new mate or lover appear in my life, or will a new effort on my behalf secure a new position or even vocation? That we cannot know at once how things will turn out, and that we are reminded with the utmost gravity that we must continue to live on in spite of the loss and sudden but permanent absence of the way things were, suggests that all of these ambiguities are both associated with death but they are also life. If they appear not in its blessed fullness, at least they remain present in its threshold hour of slack in the turning of the tide. Like this natural phenomenon that we can know as a certain return, life itself gradually rebounds in spite of the slack water of the presence of that which is no longer alive.

A second form denoting "spaces of memory" can be called "the rationalization of source." This is of particular import concerning living memory, upon which we rely so much in the absence of the deeds that traditionally make history what it is and what can be known about our own pasts. In the absence of great and glorious deeds, or the invention of objects that transform social relations and organization, or the shift in institutions that radically alter how we think and live, what is left is indeed the great bulk of history as regular people have lived it. This is the history of the unknown and unknowable, and, as the French philosopher of interpretation, Paul Ricoeur (1973 [1969]), suggests, this is in fact the true history of humankind simply because the vast majority of all of those who have ever lived are not represented in historical narrative. For this "true history," we must rely upon the individual oral narrative of living persons and their subjective experiences. Given that the source of oral narrative and hence the memory of it is often obscure, apocryphal, even aleatory, we tend to "rationalize the source" to give it an authority it otherwise would not have.

The most evident example of the rationalizing of source material is the simple act of putting someone's opinion, statement, or self as a model on a monument. Suddenly the ambiguity of the oral or obscure action is elevated into an iconography. Anything that becomes inscribed or engraved in this manner becomes part of what we can know as history. It is more likely, as seen with the sociology of science, that what actually occurred was indeed too ambiguous, its meaning vague or at least equivocal, its motives often irrational or even non-rational, to ever become significant without this rationalizing process. If oral memory is compromised by the original contexts of utterances being obscure, then the inscription of what was previously merely speech at least marginalizes these ambiguities to careful and arcane historical scholarship where it cannot intrude upon the official narrative of men of daring and immediate decision.

If this device still fails to produce a solid label for an even more solid mark of a moment of death, then what is encountered by the observer are many explanatory plaques and plates, photographs and artifacts, diaries and serious scholarship to assuage the feeling of distanciation and loss of control over our own past and our own cultural lives. The most important message of both field museums and souvenir shops is, "We can know this, you can own this, take back your history, possess control over what you are, and what we as a people have been." Plaques explain the action and decision, with much less weight given to the inaction and indecision. Books, videos, replica artifacts, are available. It is obvious that we are attempting—in the same manner as the prosthetic attempts at the prolongation of life outlined above—an artificial prolonging of the longing to be ourselves thought of as historical beings. What occurred happened without us. What is occurring happens often without our consent, which amounts to something very similar as the passing of an anonymous history. The angst created by not feeling at home in one's own history, let alone not being present for the fullness of historical being, presents to our projects of living history serious challenges at the emotional level, which, it was often observed, were transferred into the level of being accurate to the technology of the time in question, which in turn yet renders our prostheses ultimately impotent. How does one get living right yet not become too obsessed with the ability to live is a challenge all of us must face.

A third form of our second category of memorialization consists of "the replication of the lived," or the copying of that which did live and no longer lives as an original. Gadamer relates that in this case, what we are faced with is a task that from the beginning is known to be, in some sense, disingenuous:

> The final parting which death demands from those who are left behind brings about, at the same time, a transformation in the image of the dead person which the living retain in their consciousness and memory. That we should never speak ill of the dead is a prescription that can scarcely be called a prescription. It is rather an irrepressible need of human nature not only to preserve the character of the dead person, which has been transformed through permanent separation, but to reconstruct it in its productive and positive form...we come to experience their presence in a different way (1996:66–7 [1985]).

Whatever the source for this motive for and motion of replication, the cultural manifestation of the copying that was fully present as an original must assume a number of things. One, that the original indeed and in deed was worth copying. How a life is valued depends very much on its use in official histories, whether the institutional source of those histories is church, nation-state, family, or science. Two, one assumes that any mimicry would be convincing to those who knew the original person, place, or thing. There are no guarantees—however authentic to the "rightness" of history as perceived by what is not yet history and by those who are not yet deceased—that we will believe in the ongoing presence of the departed character in an optimistic imagery. We come perilously close to the "good old days" shibboleth with any vain attempt at simply stuffing the character full of whitewashed official narrative, or yet preserving the object, body, or space in the formal formaldehyde of whitewash itself. In order to replicate what life once was with a view to overcoming its absence, many diverse vehicles of the metaphor of likeness and contiguity are called into play.

Through a kind of sympathetic or even contagious magic, the proximity to an important event suddenly renders important all mundane items within the field of vision. Of course, the great medieval cathedrals as reliquaries—many built to house such magical items as bones, thorns from the crown of thorns, bits of wood from the "true" cross and the like—are the most famous examples of the magical contiguity to historic events. An event that would be accorded the highest status would, ironically, be ultimately thought of as beyond history, as a part of a series of extramundane phenomena. The death of a god might prove to be the trump in this case. However great or small the historical event is deemed to be, it is, in the absence of the actuality of that event and the lives which inhabited and constructed its actuation, the artifacts both natural and cultural that remain in mute testament to the space of the action.

Finally, rounding out the characteristics of the second category of memorialization are attempts and interpretations that "ignore the source" in favor of a more ingratiating, romantic, or politically stable take on events inherently ambiguous and fraught with the non-rational or even the irrational. This sub-form is most evident when there are events in a biography or a culture history that are difficult to explain by the transferring of empirical or archival methods across the barrier of time. That is, we ourselves would have difficulty in explicating similar phenomena if they occurred within the present. If the importing of motives based on the presumed customs "of the time" or thinly veiled as present ideology does not suffice to satisfactorily understand the event, then we tend to turn to another source that generates a more plausible event in itself. Thus paraphysical spaces of memory are either rationalized away as nonsense, or they are, somewhat perversely perhaps, celebrated in their marginality or even given an occult status. Narratives of these types of events are never wanting, peculiarly, given that their content and one's relation of such might engender stigma from a general audience. This simply suggests that only where we have artificially decided to memorialize and monumentalize death in general does one by social convention exhibit the sober respect and humility such events might inspire, once again, generally, in us. The paraphysical spaces where the remains of life lie ethereally are thus contrived.

More interesting for the living are the supposed encounters with the dead whilst oneself is yet alive. My favorite ghost story involves a Victorian house in the deep South where a girl was said to have died. Apart from the usual kinds of narratives describing the vestiges of her presence—footsteps on the stairs, pets being agitated, even feelings of almost physical contact—one part of the collection of stories stands out. For some years the house was vacant, at least of its earthly tenants. One night all of the interior lights in the house were apparently turned on. The police were called, the neighbors fearing some mischief and possible vandalism. They attempted entry, but all the doors were locked from the inside as they should have been. No sign of forced entry could be distinguished. The police then called the utilities men, rousing them from their beds around three in the morning. They duly clambered up the pole that delivered electricity to the house. When they discovered that the shunt to the brightly lit place was already off, they high-tailed it back home, as did the police!

Even if we disdain the implications of such narratives, it does sometimes seem that the source, imaginary or no, is easier to ignore in some cases than in others. Suffice to say that whatever the explanation offered, or offered as paraphysical, what this understanding of the represencing of a bit of forlorn and fragile history must satisfy is our wonder for things unknown or even unknowable. The social construction of reality must include within it the construction of the unreal as well.

The final category of memorialization, also possessing four components, is that which allows us to "rewrite histories." This is perhaps the most important ability the present has against the past, but it is also subject to much abuse. The four forms that both allow contemporaries to ignore their predecessors and proselytize their successors include: ix) "metaphoric monuments," x) "the tongues of the dead," xi) "prescience creates presence," and xii) "the illusory past self." Part of the drive to rewrite history stems not merely from vulgar ideological concerns that animate all who seek to control the history of those they seek to physically or legally coerce. There is another more pressing anxiety, perhaps underlying all elements of the attempt to control. This is simply the knowledge, as we discussed above, that we cannot empirically own our own futures. As Gadamer neatly puts it, "We can be said to have a future for as long as we are not aware that we have no future" (1996:65 [1985]). The sense that we need to ignore or even deny the fact of our universal mortality may be transferred into the apparent ability we do have in the present to control the past, at least temporarily.

That such monuments are metaphoric—that they cannot be taken literally for what they are but only as a shifting locus of currently fashionable political symbolism—means that this species of metaphor must speak to us in a known tongue. All inscriptions therefore are in the language of the living. No Rosetta Stone can translate recognizably the language of the dead. We must come to grips with the process of translation itself. We, the elite of the still living as opposed to the very marginal class of those who are not even alive, let alone disenfranchised, also may be said to perform this task either with integrity or with ignorance, or yet worse still, with deliberate manipulation.

The worst case of a people's history being manufactured remains the Third Reich, but there are today disconcertingly similar examples from around the globe. All references to Japanese involvement in the Second World War, specifically the perpetration of atrocities, has recently been expunged from all Japanese school textbooks. In the United States, depending on the region, core discursive concepts such as organismic evolution and the geological time scale disappear. Critiques of capital, of market democracy, and the sordid history of race relations are whitewashed. Ignorance of history in general, coupled with scientific ignorance, creates fertile ground for the rewriting of political and social history to suit the needs of the nation-state. The language of the living is not at all necessarily the language of all those who live.

The second motif of the "rewriting histories" structure—"dead tongues"—accentuates the first. We are missing the point of memorialization if we do not admit that the dead do not now speak a living tongue. However they may speak, the translation process is at best occlusive. This ambiguity or even deliberate mystery in some cases allows us to rewrite history to authenticate any present politics. It is correct to say that history as a whole is cut from a very narrow cloth. Not only in the sense of Ricoeur's invisible histories of those who are not part of "Historical Man" but also in the sense that what humans do and have done probabilistically bears little resemblance to the events that are memorialized as history. One might argue that, akin to news media, only the excessive and extramundane is worth recording. But to whom is the definition of the worth of history directed, and who benefits from these narrow definitions? If we assume that the purpose of memorialization is essentially political, then any other kind of analysis, even biography, may be part of the reproduction of official history as at least worth analysis and critique. The irony of all critique and satire might be the inevitable represencing of that which would ideally be changed, not as a rewritten version that attempts to escape from blame or bad conscience, but as a present factor that abets suffering or injustice.

This reflection leads us immediately to the third component of the final category of memorialization, that which I have called "prescience creates presence." Akin to posterity, the interpretation that allows for historical figures to speak again in a living language as prescient of the future impact of their once contemporary actions creates a new presence. The most common manifestation of this illusory kinship with predecessors occurs in the trivialization of history. Historical knowledge most often appears in the mundane as questions and answers on game shows, for instance, or to "know history" might become the knowledge of the petty pedigrees of popular culture figures in the world of sports and entertainment. Yet the trivialization of history, either by the picayune way history is taught in public schools across North America—facts, dates, statistics rather than themes, structures, discourses—or by its cameo appearance within popular culture as yet more facts and dates, is still a manner of remembering. It may indeed be the most common trait of memorialization. If so, the insignificant space it is granted as a means to vulgar ends mirrors the eventuality that very few actual facts compared to the sheer immensity of historical knowledge extant get airtime, even if they do so repeatedly. Only when board games and game shows have elite stakes—large monetary prizes, for example—do we see an extension of the challenge to know history in greater detail, if not in greater depth.

This mode of recollection of the trivial serves another purpose than to impress one's peers with one's capacity for the so-called "general knowledge" or to win money on television. History represented as a staccato of disconnected facts, figures, and dates can never provide a thematic continuity that would help us to understand structural variables and their current presence and force in our own society. Knowledge of history is, in fact, to know ourselves as living history, and what we have lived through as history. From an hermeneutic point of view, historicity then is never attained, let alone effective historical consciousness. From an ideological point of view, such a trivial pursuit of historical facts remains very convenient.

Yet there may be an even deeper reason for the prescient trivialization of history. Presumably, it is bound up with that inner connection already described between life and the repression of death that the knowledge that we ourselves must die remains almost veiled, even when, as mature adults, this knowledge has become established at the deepest inner level within us. And even then, when the clearest and most express knowledge of approaching death makes itself felt and can no longer be concealed, the will to life and the will towards the future is known to be so strong in some people that they are not even prepared to complete the legal requirements of a last testament (Gadamer 1996:65 [1985]).

Similarly, those who do not wish to commit to organ donation, affixing labels on the reverse of driver's licenses and the like, may be attempting to negotiate reality in these terms. The teaching and using of historical facts as disconnected trivia may indeed be a disguised form of the "will to life." If so, it is misplaced, because its effects hinder social maturity towards better quality of life for all persons, and thus ironically predestines many to fates that may be kindred to living deaths. Once again, this motif is prescient of the ultimate state of all human futures. It brings forward in time the presence of death and forces one to live as if that present had arrived prematurely.

The final sub-form of the third category of memorialization—"the illusory past self"—outlines the other major model of our relationship to history, the other formula that the present uses to negotiate both its specific past and the past in general. Rewriting the self's existence as illusory is akin to all historical romance. If one witnesses the trivialization of history in popular culture and in school, one also must confront the sentimentalization of history in other vicarious social realms. The historical novel, the historical quotations on signage at national historical monuments, and the exotic travel literature that purports to be both ethnography and fashion—these are spaces of this form of memorialization. Even holiday photographs or videos of mundane outings perform this final function. What occurred cannot, in the linear conception of temporality, ever occur again. From photograph to re-enactment, the attempt to arrest the flow of linear time marshals much of our personal resources. The interiors of people's homes become personal museums.

The rewriting of the self's existence as illusory may indeed have this doubling effect. On the one hand, the selves that existed in the past provide the illusions of sense of self in the present. At the same time, the present self retreats into its own version of history as a kind of "autohagiography," the killing of the past self through either a whitewashed or aggrandized autobiography. This suggests, on the other hand, that when individuals memorialize what they label as their own history, they themselves become historical and lose touch with the reality of the present. It may be so that such a reality is too intolerable to confront each day, and thus the represencing of historical spaces as veritable time machines is understandable, if not particularly constructive. Yet when a society memorializes its own history, it does so primarily to support a version of the present that is often precisely the source of the oppressions individuals suffer.

There remains one final function that characterizes any set of categories of memorialization, although it cannot be said to occur within its list of categories By haunting the mental and physical topologies of being with both famous and anonymous historical figures, we attempt to memorialize the very space in which our present living being must exist. Although famous figures populate official narratives of memorialization, and anonymous ones are often the grist for paraphysical or occult personal narratives of remembering, these spaces of both contrived or spontaneous recall allow the living to gradually ingratiate themselves with the dead with whom they will have, sooner or later, a more intimate intercourse.

Categories of memorialization, whether serving ideological masters or personal demons, conjuring tragedy or heroism, drudgery or romance, take the present living as the future dead. All forward looking beings must complete the circle of life, whose torus is often gradual enough that we do not notice that we are returning to our places of origin. It may be that "at this limit a true solidarity of all mankind with one another is expressed in so far as we all recognize and acknowledge this mystery. Whoever lives must accept death. We are all border-crossers at the limit between this world and the beyond" (Gadamer 1996:67 [1985]). There are as many ways of recognizing this universal limit on human life as there are of attempting to avoid it. The nature of mortal memory contains at least the twelve versions we have discussed so far. Their pattern is not set to one particular use or abuse. Nostalgia itself can be seen as an optimistic and future-looking style of memory that wishes to reproduce not so much the reality of the past, but its quaintness and perhaps its perspective. Hardly anyone would truthfully say that they would desire to live in the world as it was even fifty years ago, although each of us as we grow older might well wonder where our "lost youth" has gone. Was it history itself that absconded with it? The replication of most of the same kinds of social events in our children's generation is wont to remind us that things do not change as much as they seem to stay the same. Yet one can wonder if it is only in our more experienced eyes that things look the same. For younger persons, everything in the world is new. Each experience has not been had before. The entire idea of "before" is truncated to a mere insignificance when seen only with a child's memory. This may be why we assume that only vivid experiences have any effect on changing the ways of children, too wilful or too obedient as the case may be.

The function of having a memory at all is to prepare us to negotiate what is to come. The present must be recognized for what it is, and the perspective of the past is the only framework with which we have to perform accurately and with foresight in the day-to-day. The relationship between experience that has both been reflected upon and archived as a worthy memory, and what will occur to us in the morrow is the essence of life as work. Here, work must be taken in the sense of a "life's work," and not mere labor. Life, correspondingly, must be taken in its fullest sense, not in a manner that is merely sentient or conscious. Sometimes we regard with both pride and suspicion the evolutionary gift of human intelligence, and speak therefore of "intelligent life." It makes sense that we desire a fuller understanding of this oddly fragile and finite intelligence that seeks worlds beyond itself. Could it be that we are a part of something much greater than ourselves or our species? This something would only have the appearance of a self-contained biological ancestry. Life would only appear to end, and death would be only the outward manifestation of a true rite of passage, one through which a new life is granted us, or some version of what it had been.

The following chapters will explore each of the major versions of this bold and perhaps desperate idea. Such an idea ultimately suggests that, rather than life being merely the "most interesting part of death," as Nietzsche puts it, might it as likely be that death is the most interesting part of life, as it is its shadowy threshold that propels two very different forms of living side by side, vessels of consciousness passing close by in the sudden night of starless firmament.

2
Types of Belief Regarding the Afterlife
Part 1: Unevaluated Return

> *Whatever the religious conceptions of life and death were like which animated the cults surrounding death in the different phases of our early history, there is nevertheless one thing they have in common. They all testify to the fact that humankind neither wanted nor was able to admit that the dead were no longer here, that they had departed, that they finally no longer belonged.*
>
> —Hans-Georg Gadamer

The most ancient type of belief concerning the character of the afterlife is that of an immediate and unevaluated return to the living. What does this mean? Consider the common sensibility of the importance of ancestry. Its relevance may be claimed regarding physical appearance, talent or proclivity, personality or character. Lately, the most relevant aspect of one's pedigree is the history of the health of the family tree concerning genetic illness and risk of developing certain debilitating conditions. There are all kinds of tests one may undergo to determine the likelihood of this or that condition ensuing, or if already in its onset, the chances of our survival. Much of this is taken to be the consequence of our interest in the probability of longevity and quality of life given what our ancestors underwent. The idea of a family history being of interest to our medical doctors can mean only this one point, rather than the exploits or foibles of one's great aunts and uncles. The complete mapping of the human genome, a major scientific milestone in the history of our species, all but ensures the continued interest in the biological history of the vectors of inherited disease and lack thereof. All manner of questions are both raised and resolved by such a feat of genetics. Those who carry the HIV virus and yet never develop AIDS are seen to have some kind of inherited insulation, the key to which is of obvious interest to the rest of us.

Similarly for all sorts of diseases, both environmental and genetic, our interest lies in the potential ability not merely to cure illnesses but to prevent them by extinguishing the genetic possibility that they should ever again exist. The shadowy side of such efforts may also be obvious to us, such as the eugenics-inspired search for the "superior race"—the consequences of this idea should still be fresh in our historical consciousness. As with all human knowledge, the use and valuation of it depends mightily on both the individual conscience of the person within this or that society as well as the moral suasion of that same society. Stem cell research and the ability to produce replacement body parts for diseased ones no doubt improves the lot of individuals but could also be said to "improve" the general lot of the species as a whole. The engineering of human genetic strings bereft of deleterious alleles or genes has within it also the great promise of a better world yet perhaps also the danger of the perennial idea that strength, health, beauty, and longevity are inherently superior to other forms of apparently "truncated" human life. This duet of sensibilities, the one that wishes to overcome suffering for all humanity, and the one that says that some human life is unworthy of life and thus must be overcome, is inherited by us not through our genes, but through our beliefs about the influence of the dead. Most specifically, the dead that are related to us as individual persons are the ancestors of interest to us.

This interest is not merely egotistical. That is, it does not of necessity center on how we feel about our chances of the best life possible. It is also about our questions regarding why we are alive in the first place, and what, given the fact of our living existence, it may mean to ourselves and others that we are alive, rather than not. The idea that some persons live much longer than others is also suggestive to us. We regularly cite the person's ancestry as a kind of evidence for the fact of their longevity. "His ancestors were long-lived," we might say, or "She must have good genes" are common remarks. What exactly does "good" mean in this instance? Both quantity and quality of life are at issue here. We might well distrust the medical establishment when it trumpets the call for things like stem cell research given that we are also aware of all the times a terminally ill relative or friend wishes to depart from this world without further ado, much less more medical mischief that prolongs only life's quantities and thus in a sense degrades the dignity of human life. Perhaps the seemingly irrational calls to halt scientific research into genetics and human evolution stem from the suspicion that we may be yet more beholden to medical practice and worldview at the expense of how we feel about who we are as a living being, and what has made our life worthwhile. Certainly, given today's technology, I would strongly be inclined to accept death once my intellectual and authorial skills have vanished, as no doubt at some point they will, and if they are not supplanted by some other set of worthwhile and constrictive abilities. Indeed, the judgement of what is of worth must be left to the person involved, and cannot become enshrined in some kind of external doctrine, medical or otherwise. The anxiety about the placement of moral discourse is what likely lies at the heart of such controversies such as stem cell research and the like, rather than a blind opposition to science for its own sake, irrational or non-rational as may be the source.

All of this serves to put up a signpost as to the stakes that may be involved with our notion of ancestry and our presumed connections of the living to the dead. The dead may not reach out and grasp us in the manner of the mischievous morgue, but it does seem like their grasp is not entirely withdrawn upon passing. We do inherit both strengths and weaknesses from our forebears, and as everyone who has applied for life insurance is aware, some weaknesses are more dangerous than others. Actuarial tables aside, it is common knowledge that the probability of a lengthy and healthy life depends to a fair extent on the health of one's ancestors, and as the vast majority of these are long dead and have left no records for us to gauge our odds, it makes sense for us to both harbor anxiety about our individual fates—part of a more general existential anxiety—and to be immediately interested in being able to ignore our family history and rewrite it, as it were, much in the same manner as rewriting our memories, as we saw in Chapter One.

The genetic rewriting of our original inheritance, or yet the stem cell replacement of our original body parts makes eminent sense in so far as parts can be damaged in accidents and, as no one asks to be born, one would think it reasonable to eliminate genetic deficits of all kinds. The ethical problem arises when one steps over the threshold of death back into life. By this I mean that "designer babies" have the hallmarks of value judgements that are made about the living. Esthetics, physical prowess, even body shape and size are all characteristics which in life are fully negotiable as values, but which in the past were actualities. Now that we have the technology to alter these kinds of non-life-threatening variables, we must confront the difference once again between what might be reasonably applied as necessary or even just, and what is merely the whim or fancy of fashion—or worse, of fascism.

Yet this is a relatively simple problem when compared with the other confrontation that genetic engineering brings about. Replacing the parts of a prematurely damaged or ill person seems rational and just. What, however, is the definition of premature? Echoing Poe's homiletic, we do not wish to go to grave "before our time." Yet this kind of sentiment only begs the question. What is "our" time? When is it? We generally use two rubrics when we judge the timing of the deaths of others, and also then anticipate our own. One is a social fact, a pattern of behavior and event that is external to our wishes and is larger than belief. It is external to what we would personally like to see in the world because it is made up of many millions of individual cases that describe the biographic events of other human beings. It is larger than belief because, although perhaps hundreds of millions of us worldwide share some basic beliefs about life and death, the statistical tables that construct social facts have no cultural or historical limit. Mortality rates, suicide rates—about which we shall have much more to say in the final chapter—and crime rates are examples of social facts. These facts are as real as those revealed by the sciences that explore nature as a whole. They are descriptive and empirical in the most transparent sense. But their real relevance is not suggested by the word "fact," but rather the word "social." It is we who make up the social facts, while engaging in social behavior and acting upon social beliefs. So, when we are witness to a funeral, we can easily make the judgement regarding what is "premature" and what is not, simply by referring to our general knowledge of common ages and causes of death, tables of which are regularly published and readily available. It is obvious to us that—barring a sudden and previously hidden genetic switch going off—that if someone dies at age thirty, this death would be regarded as premature, even tragic. If someone is ninety and has only the illnesses of old age to account for and dies in their sleep, it would be a rare individual who would mourn such a loss as tragic in itself, even if the biography as a whole contained many tragic events. Now that there are no more "hidden switches" inside of us like alien saboteurs ready to blow us away, we quite rationally suppose that we can judge the timing of others' deaths all the more appropriately.

The other rubric we use in evaluating the justness or the justice of the event of death has precisely to do with whether or not the life that has been lived is deemed worthy of the death. I often remind my students at the end of term to "make their lives worth dying for." This bit of perhaps melodramatic homily is usually well taken, as university students are most often of the age where mortality first enters their consciousness in the sense that they have experienced enough of life to at least know that they are themselves not immortal. The adolescent obliviousness to the fragility of living beings is wearing off, and persons are ready to look to the future in a manner that is suggestive of finiteness. No longer is there the inchoate presence of a life that carries on indefinitely, but instead of one where things must be accomplished and one is placed on an existential schedule. Mostly the "deadlines" of this new schedule come from institutions and peer groups. Are young persons going to have children and marry? If so, when and with whom? Are they going to complete their education by a certain time—the North American average for undergraduate degrees is about six years—and above all else, how are they going to find a job, much a less a career?

Not that any of these events, impositions, and ambitions force us to confront our own deaths. What they do accomplish is a reorientation in our sense of time from the present to the future. We are always "looking ahead," perhaps until we retire. By that time, of course, the much more immanent specter of dying and death refocuses our thoughts once again. This is why I exhort students not to wait until they have lived the bulk of their life—potentially in jobs and even unions that are unfulfilling—before they begin to reflect on such questions as "What have I done with my life?"

If we are once again present at a funeral of someone we judge to have "wasted" his life in some way, our mourning is potentially filled with a double regret. We mourn the loss of the person who did not fulfill his or her dreams or was thwarted in the attempt by other forces—perhaps including the social facts of certain illnesses and irrecoverable accidents that human genome and stem cell research is designed to resolve—as well as feeling the example of loss as our own. Have we lived up to our abilities? Have we done what needed to be done in life? Is there enough time left to us to adjust our courses if the responses are negative? If we decide that we have not been fulfilled and that we cannot be, we may be said to have "given up" on life, which is also an ethical event that can induce tremendous regret. Hence the combination of an objective judgement based on the factuality of demographic rates and an ethical judgement based on a subjective evaluation of the life of others and of our own allows us to understand a death as untimely or as appropriate.

Yet it is in regret that the key to our first conception of the afterlife may be found. If mourning itself is the origin of all memories, as the French sociologist Emile Durkheim suggested long ago, it may be that the earliest human societies were driven to conceive of an afterlife that addressed the dual problem of demographics and ethics. On the one hand, the loss of any member of such a small-scale society would be felt intimately by the whole. This was one clue to Durkheim's understanding of what he called "mechanical solidarity." This idea assumes that in tiny bands of hunters and gatherers every person would not only know what each other knew in terms of experience and survival, subsistence and socialization, but also what everyone knew about beliefs and values. In such social organizations, there could be no conflict of interpretations over what mattered, or else such a small-scale society would fly apart, never to recover. Indeed, it was in the concept of what could constitute a crime in such a culture that originally gave Durkheim the clue he needed to advance the notion of what he called the "collective conscience," a value system where each member of the society in question would think exactly like the other members with regard to belief and ethic. It seems to us today, living in the very polar opposite of such a system—Durkheim called modern society "organic" based on the idea that it was an interrelated system of unlike parts and as such could not help but have conflicts over values and beliefs—that the collective conscience would almost be telepathic in quality. Nostalgia may yearn for such a golden age of human social organization, and some of the greatest thinkers of modern society certainly did so, Rousseau and Marx included, but Durkheim simply stated it as an anthropological fact long past and not necessarily relevant to the contemporary era. At the same time, he cautioned that if human society lost all sense of collective conscience it would inevitably perish.

The loss of a like part of a collective would, on the other hand, call into question the existence of a small scale society with a conscience that was shared so intimately amongst its members. For us today, a loss of another human being represents a personal loss, and much more rarely do we speak of a loss to our culture or society as a whole. That occurs only when some famous person has dedicated their life to the public good; in other words, to the collective soul of what we imagine ourselves to ideally be. This in itself is a resonance of the original social contract by which humanity developed in the first place. In mechanical solidarity, each loss would be as if one had lost part of one's own body, a limb or a sense organ, for each part was a number in an equation that added up only to the sum of its parts, and the gestalt of early human social organization was found in its behaving more akin to a flock of birds on the wing, or a school of fish adjusting its underwater course. Not that Durkheim was suggesting that "primitive" humans were more like animals than ourselves. Quite to the contrary—he was one of the few thinkers of the fin de siècle period who felt that there was no difference in cognitive ability and apparatus across any culture made up of the same species. Yet intimacy and the lack of any diversity in the division of labor and within social role expectations brought human beings closer than they were ever to be again.

Even in modern forms of intimacy, we are very conscious of not merely differences of opinion, which all couples endure, but of real and serious differences in values and even purpose of life. This was apparently not the case for human societies until beginning about twenty thousand years ago, and then only in very specific regions of the earth. It was the advent of agriculture some ten millennia ago that brought a more definite shift in human consciousness. This shift was pronounced in its suasion that there were different sorts of human beings extant on earth at the same time, with correspondingly different fates—but more on that in the next chapter. For denizens of mechanical societies, the loss of a fellow member was felt as a loss of oneself. Every other person of the tribal group died with the physical death of the one. Durkheim's ethnographic sources are now considered to be both dated and suspect, but the descriptive accounts of death and mortuary rites amongst Stone Age societies remain relevant even if Victorian interpretations of them may not. That there was a fetish, a desire for the seeming liberation of the exotic and "primitive" during Durkheim's day, cannot be denied, but at the same time such a keen interest provoked an earnestness and honesty in documenting the events of societies which appeared to Europeans to be from a time that time itself had forgotten.

The deaths of fellow human beings in intimate small-scale settings were felt to be cataclysmic events, and were marked as such with a wildness and a raw and primordial transparency that would be quite foreign to anything we know in the world today. Apart from self-mutilation and general all-in assault, the mimicry of the deaths of totemic animals was performed with a relish and a keenness that would mark the finest drama. If one was a member of the snake clan, for instance, and a fellow snake had perished, the writhing and twisting of the animal would be performed lying on the ground, and the characteristic marks in the sand or earth of the death throes of the reptile would appear underneath its human cousin. For it was not that these people felt their relationship with nature to be mere analogy, as we might with an affiliation to an agrarian zodiacal sign—as a "horse" on the Chinese zodiac, for instance, I am supposedly gregarious and need intimate company, quite true—but rather their relationship was one of homology. That is, the same structure animated the life force in both the snake and the human of that totem or clan. Thus when either a fellow snake died, or when what we would call a real snake died, and its death was actually noticed by a human being, similar rites might be performed. When a member of a pre-agrarian society says, "I am a snake, eagle, raven" or what-have-you, he really means it not as a likeness, but as a statement of the utmost empiricality. The "personality" of these animals, suggested by their behavior and the human imagination, is what is embodied in the person who is of their kind.

It is not so much that traditional peoples live "closer" to nature, as is often said by anthropologists and environmentalists alike. The advent of the social contract forever severed the instinctual ties that bind animal consciousness to the wider cosmos of the natural world. Our kind of consciousness is something that is primarily learned, has the capabilities of reflection and foresight, and, as we have seen, of memory generating a concept of the differences of time, past, present, and future. The proximity of human culture to nature is manifest rather in subsistence strategies and relatively simple technologies of resource extraction. Population loads were so slight during the vast majority of human tenure on earth that the biosphere was never seriously threatened by human activities. All of the crises of human life and the fate of the planet with which we are so currently familiar are of recent origin. This alone may have given rise to the equally current mythology that human beings from pre-agrarian cultures were somehow "naturally" superior to ourselves, or were "born environmentalists." This is a fallacy both of observation and of ethics. Resources were used simply by what was necessary for social reproduction, and the supply always far outweighed the demand.

By "necessary" however, we do not mean that all of these groups led Spartan or Amish-like lifestyles, eschewing the glamour or conspicuous consumption that characterizes later human social formations. It is clear from the historical and ethnographic records that only truly mechanical societies had no forms of private property and displays of wealth, hence once again the interest that enlightenment and post-enlightenment social reformers showed in these groups. Even the idea that traditional societies respected nature is not quite correct. They believed that they were a part of nature, whereas we tend to be insulated from this idea, living as we do apart from nature and in the midst of technological culture. The fear or respect engendered by recognizing that nature was different from culture comes about only much later, with the beginnings of sedentary society and agricultural practices. Rather, early human groups made no such distinction in their beliefs, even though we have already seen that to be human is to be cultural and social in a way that is utterly distinct from the instinctual animal natures, even those which do in fact exhibit much learned and therefore social, behavior.

Given all of this, the belief that originates in this seemingly primitive form of human social organization that is most salient for a discussion of the afterlife can be called "unevaluated return." By this I mean that the members of such societies believed that a "pool of souls" or animating life-forces existed as part of the world around them. The prevailing belief system might have been animistic—all things have a kind of consciousness or life force, best recently seen in Buddhism—in which forces of nature were personified or given anthropomorphic qualities as in the much later Scandinavian religions. The beliefs might have been totemic, which as we have already seen, links specific animals or other natural "events" with particular groups of people. In either case, the pool of souls would be larger or smaller, shared by either the universe of soul or specific categories thereof. What really matters is, however, that when one dies, his spirit is more or less immediately returned through the birth of another being. If a member of the snake clan passes, her soul might reappear in an actual snake, or in some other newborn member of that same clan. If the pool is much more broad, then one's animus might find itself animating a river or part of a forest, etc.

If one key characteristic is that the soul returns to the same world upon the death of its late host, then the other key element is that this return is unevaluated. This means simply that whatever has passed between the host and its soul during this life or some other is not subject to any kind of measure, ranking, or judgement. The spirit simply returns to a kindred host. We will see in the following chapter that the kernel of this idea is given measure with what has been called reincarnation. Yet the reincarnative qualities of these more ancient beliefs did not originally have such trappings. The likely reason why mechanical pre-agrarian groups developed the conception of unevaluated return was that there existed no hierarchies in their societies, and no real way to make comparative measures amongst the acts that occur or are calculated throughout the life course of different persons. Not only were persons not thought of as "different" from one another in any individuated sense, there were also no specialized roles or divisions of labor. The lack of conflict regarding value systems and beliefs further fostered the sensibility that one person's soul was not only exchangeable through death with some other host, but that these souls, within certain totemic or animistic categories, were interchangeable.

It is this element of our first conception of the afterlife that has no serious current reference. Reincarnation is something well known to us, though we may not hold it as a belief, and even the idea of the lack of judgement has recently once again become important to parts of our culture. But we today hold our souls to be unique, if we imagine that we possess a soul at all. What we are is manifestly not the same as what someone else is, and this almost ideological subjectivity certainly extends to the other world, whatever it might consist of. This was not the case for earlier human societies, and clearly, beliefs that animated the afterlife for these peoples reflected not only their social organization and division of labor, but also the lack of conflict concerning both material resources and the symbolic order that gave ultimate meaning to their lives. Each member of a mechanical solidarity was interchangeable as a fully functioning citizen and cultural repository. That their spirits were interchangeable in death is thus no surprise, even though it is an idea that is radically different from our own. Just as with some of the folk beliefs of our own direct ancestors, however, these early cultures shared the idea that if a death and a birth occurred closely together in the calendar, that it was likely that the spirit of whomever had just passed would return to inhabit the new life just come into the world. In a very real sense then, all "new" life has been here before, and what is new is not so much what gives life, but what holds it, temporarily, until its hostel too is replaced over time with the passing of each subsequent and serial vessel of the living. When we with much less seriousness suggest that a newborn has the looks of his grandfather and joke that he may well share his personality as well as he grows older, it is a resonance of one of most ancient conceptions of life and death known to us.

Yet there are other stronger reminders of what at first seems to be an idea of the afterlife foreign to our own beliefs. If return itself has not entirely been extinguished by the overlay of more recent conceptions of the afterlife, and the sense that there may be a lack of judgement concerning our passage from death back into life is also something, ironically, that has been "born again" of late, then we have at least understood the interchangeability of the pool of souls in our own more individuated manner. At first glance there seem to be three well-known phenomena that remind us of the mechanical conceptions of life and death. The first is an extension of the rewriting of our experiences in light of the needs of the day, through a number of the modes of memorialization discussed in the first chapter. These are the personal fables we tell ourselves about why we do things the way we do, or why the elements of our character as we understand them have come to be. When I was very young, before a living memory took hold that I can recall as an adult, my parents said I enjoyed telling people that I had "secret orange eyes," apropos of either nothing at all or sometimes prompted by persons commenting on my manifestly chocolate brown orbs. What reference I could have taken this from is unknown to me, but one supposes that I had heard something as a toddler that provoked this statement. As my family name means "lions," with the German Mennonite spelling, I much later used to joke that I had been reincarnated from a real lion, a beast that most often has orange eyes. The sense that my early self had seemingly come up with such an outré statement from thin air lent some fabulous credibility to the outlandish idea that one's spirit could be interchangeable with not only any other human being, but other forms of consciousness as well.

This fable is precisely alike to the conception of the mechanical afterlife. It, along with uncounted other versions of the personal narrative we tell ourselves—likely only-half seriously, if that—are what animate our lives in that they give us an extended meaningfulness to the everyday and lend purpose to our existence. It is no surprise that for the earliest of human cultures, these kinds of now idiosyncratic stories were elevated into mythology and culture as a whole. Quite apart from the color of my eyes, either in this life or in those "past," everyone who knows me knows that I play on the lion theme in a number of other ways that cast my personality as having that of the anthropomorphized big cat. Of course, I share with my fellow humans the penchant for choosing only the best or most noble traits of this or that animal or other natural phenomenon and downplaying the more savage or even ruthless elements of what we might imagine a lion's "character" to be. That is one of the chief privileges of concocting a personal fable: the complete ability to manipulate the facts of the matter to suit one's self-image and to reconstruct one's self-esteem. That we are regularly faced with the all-too-human world of solid social and empirical facts is sometimes too much for us and we need to retreat. This respite is necessary if only for a little while, and we may egress from the adult world into the pleasant imaginings of the young child whose own "soul," if you will, has remained inside of us as both a sense of misadventure but also as a charming guide who has not lost his sense of adventure.

If we travel from the most subjective of the three ideas which hearken the return of ancient tropes and their narratives—the tall tales of childhood which are yet necessary for us to be mature in our own way and not merely as a cog in the social machine—to more generally recognized and experienced subjectivities, we arrive at the second way in which modern life still understands something of the earliest human beliefs concerning the afterlife. This is the sense that we have either been in a place before, though we have no conscious recollection of it; have performed some action or been an actor in a series of living events, commonly known as déjà vu, the "already seen"; or yet have dreamed that we have been to a place and/or acted in a certain manner and in fact consciously can recall the fact of the dreamscape. As all three of these kinds of events are usually judged as abnormative to the usual flow of time and experience, what are we to make of them both as experiences that have their explanation in the way in which human cognition works, but also in the light of our first type of afterlife?

The simplest form of déjà vu occurs when we suddenly find we recognize an event or a series of events, usually mundane, to have occurred before in our lives but without having the usual sense that "before" has meant that one has a memory of them. That is, it is not recollection that colors the perception of events, as when we might commute to work day after day, but that we have been engaged precisely and exactly in the same acts and events. This kind of déjà vu is common enough, and in fact it rather argues against the idea of unevaluated return, or for that matter, return of any interchangeable sort, because the feeling is overpoweringly strong that it was myself, in my present condition, that acted in this manner before. So much does this feeling make an impression on us that we are able to predict what will happen when we are engaged in the series of events that is colored by déjà vu. Yet the two keys to understanding this phenomena are on the one hand its very mundanity, and on the other, our apparent ability to predict.

Déjà vu occurs when we do not have a conscious memory of doing something like what we are doing beforehand, simply because what we are usually doing when we sense this extramundane quality is so routine that we in fact have likely done it many times before and in the same manner as we are now doing it. In this sense, déjà vu is a manner in which the mind keeps us from becoming complacent about regular activities—the odd feeling that we have done exactly this and we know what is coming alerts other parts of our consciousness and senses to what in fact may appear unexpectedly—and is thus likely an evolutionary adaptation. The seeming ability to predict the future during déjà vu corresponds to our sense that once again we have performed the future in the past. The déjà vu "style" of recollection is a kind of memory that does not call itself forth "from the past," as it were, but rather places itself alongside the present like a shadow that falls alongside an object. The memory is itself in the present, and acts as if it were also of the present, so we experience the characteristic "double exposure" of having already been.

The one kind of return that déjà vu might be seen as evidence for is, of course, what Nietzsche called the "eternal return of the same." This is an ancient trope in our mythology, and many scholars, including the great thinker of religious ideas, Mircea Eliade, have discussed it, but this idea descends to us not from mechanical societies but from great irrigation and agricultural mythic narratives. Notwithstanding its historical origin, the "eternal return of the same" posits that upon passing, our lives simply begin all over again, with precision and exactitude of every detail. We repeat the same existence an infinite number of times, and during this repetition, we once in awhile are exposed to its overlays in our conscious mind through events such as déjà vu. Our sensibilities about living and learning, which have their origins in the idea that life is both unique and uniquely evaluated by higher beings or the structure of the cosmos itself upon our deaths—the more common expressions of agrarian belief systems—demands that we reject eternal recurrence. Indeed, the idea rather falls flat for us, as one would wonder what the point of such an unending and unchanging cycle might be. At the same time, the eternal return of the same is not only an idea which hails from a culture different from our own, and may be accepted modestly along those lines, it also provides for us an ethics about living on which has its own merit.

Nietzsche was the most famous thinker to propound the sensibility that one must live as if life consisted of eternal recurrence, saying "yes" to life with the stiffest of jaws, not merely accepting what occurs to us but celebrating it to the extent that we would adore the God that conferred eternal return upon us. At the same time as denying any relevance of death—life simply goes on (and on) in its return—the eternal recurrence of the same disallows any evaluation. One simply lives and then lives again. In this, the ethics of a celebrated life puts itself forward as the highest form of humanity in love with its finitude. For in this view of "indefinite" life—different from the one we shall discuss in the epilogue—one wills life so heartily that one would gladly leap into another round of the same life and live again in this way unceasingly. Thus Nietzsche's notion of *amor fati*, or the love of one's fate, is inextricably linked to his sense of the ethical implications of eternal return. Although nowhere does Nietzsche speak of what is properly referred to as déjà vu, this viewpoint would allow such a phenomenon to take its place alongside other celebratory elements of the will to life. The sense that we have done something before in exactly the same way as it is transpiring now, before the very eyes of the present, tells us that we desire to will our lives with such force that we give even the mundane sphere an excess of sensibility. It is this excess that we in turn sense as having "doubled" our experience.

However unlikely any of this may be—and Nietzsche does not set up so much a metaphysics of life as he is interested in calling our attention to what the mortal and manifestly unrepeated character of the human condition ethically implies for us—the two other forms of prior perceptual experience can be taken more strongly as "evidence" that we have somehow experienced these events before without having a conscious memory of them. The second form has to do with visiting a place that to one's knowledge one has never been, and feeling most strongly that one has returned to it from having been elsewhere. We can dwell on this experience for a moment as the third form—the recollection of a dream that in its turn turns out to be predictive of reality can be seen as a variant of prior perception that locates the origin of memory in the parallax of the dreamscape. Indeed, if we imagine that the stuff of dreams must have had its origin in the stuff of life, then it is the dream itself that presents the "return," and not our actual real-time fulfillment of it. It is common enough that we hear reports that persons, upon traveling to what is taken to be a new place and having new experiences, have instead found themselves ensconced in what seems to be a memory. Did we come to this place in early childhood, perhaps, without our parents ever mentioning it to us? Did we see this place on television at an early age without recalling it or making the connection until now? Did we imaginatively project such a place or experience in our dreams that, as the vast majority of dreams go, were not recalled upon waking? In fact, given only these three options, it is most likely that one or the other holds the key to the apparent memory of what "could not have occurred" in this life. The source of apparent prior perception is probably found inside one of these options, but we cannot ignore the implications of these experiences for our beliefs regarding the nature of the afterlife.

Akin to déjà vu, prior perception—the "predictive dream," for instance—as well as recollection of that which cannot be recalled, as with "I have been here before," or "It feels like I am coming home," (a feeling, by the way, which I myself have had on a number of occasions when there was no possible way that I could have been to the places in question) are suggestive of the concept of both the eternal return of the same as well as that of the alternate "past life." Akin to having somebody else's memory suddenly thrust upon you, we might imagine that we are recalling something from a life in which our consciousness or spirit has taken part, but not as ourself. Some other person's life has been lived by what now constitutes our own consciousness. This interpretation much more closely resembles that of the subject of this chapter, the concept of unevaluated return. It is not limited to this concept, however, as the topic of the following chapter, evaluated return, might also be included in its ambit, depending perhaps on our ethical proclivities.

On at least two occasions, I have been subject to such experiences: when I resettled in Mississippi and just before I came to interview in Saskatoon, my present home. The first experience occurred when by happenstance I encountered the town in which I was to live for almost three years, driving into it through the rural back roads. It felt like a homecoming in an uncanny way. Later on I discovered that some of my neighbors were distantly related to me, having descended from the part of my family that had come to Mississippi, splitting from their intimate kin, some of whom went to Ontario. Yet this fact alone was hardly as interesting as the original feeling that I had lived in this place, or that at the very least I was to live there and I already knew it at the first moment. The second incident occurred before I was interviewed for my current position. I had a dream where I was being driven through a snowy intersection in a downtown that I did not recognize. I had never been there before. During my actual interview process, I experienced the same scene in exact detail as had "occurred" prior to it in a dream. I was so struck by this that I even took the risk of mentioning this to the person who was driving me around, who was also on the hiring committee. Fortunately it did not appear to prejudice the process.

Neither of these experiences, quite common if not commonplace, is related in order to suggest that what consciousness must be is a permutation of memories that have real historical referents that defy the standard and linear flow of time. We are aware that our conceptions of time itself are historical constructions—many science fiction and fantasy novels weave into their plots the convenience of non-linear temporality—but we are also at once aware that whatever time may be objectively, the relative time in which we live and experience history does not of its own accord run backwards or leap forwards without some kind of human reinterpretation which is impossibly subjective in scope. That is, no experience of altered temporality can be said to consist of the apparent alteration alone. It must rather also subsist upon whatever feelings and biographical experience with which we are laden at the moment in question, and thus it becomes difficult to sort out what we think may have occurred and our interpretation of the event, from any "real" change in the way the world appears to work. It is also possible, of course, that the appearance of death itself might be resolved along these same lines. In other words, that we comprehend the physicality of the deceased in a different way than does the deceased person himself.

The idea that memory must be of an event that happened or is to come is likely a cultural bias stemming from the kind of time we are used to inhabiting. We will speak more about different kinds of human history in the next chapter, but suffice to say for the moment that if we know time only as linear, then we are more apt to imagine that memory must also be linear, since it is always memory of certain events that occur within that kind of time. Thus the usual form of having an experience and recalling that experience, however rewritten and altered by the passage of yet more time and experience, is transposed by events or feelings that seem to be abnormative or contrary to the usual flow of lived time. We then think that we are recalling a prior event by extending the notion of what could be "prior" for us back into other lives which are themselves part of objective history and of course still remain "past" for ourselves. If we experience a series of events which seems to be "predictive," then we can resolve this apparent paradox by imagining that linear time runs forward and we are recalling something that has already occurred and we have lived through but in some other time line, equally linear but given a faster pace, or that we ourselves have inexplicably switched time lines either during our own present life or in some past life. Thus "predictive" events give the impression that we have lived our life before, in the manner of the eternal return of the same. Or at the very least, that we have lived our life before with certain alterations but also with certain other events remaining the same as they were.

All of this can easily become nonsense—if it is not so already—if we hold too closely to the idea that time itself must be a certain way just because our culture thinks this is the way it is. Yet the rational explanations of such abnormative events also cede nothing to alternative versions of temporality. The idea that we had dreamed of our arrival and presence in a place and recall it as a real memory situates itself within linear time. The idea that we had been to a place or had an experience in early childhood that we do not consciously recall also assumes the same. The idea that we had seen something on television or in some other media but do not consciously recall it is an attempt to resolve the issue within the concept of time that we are culturally accustomed to. Unless we adopt the notion that we do understand the nature of time correctly and this is proven by the fact that both our rational and "irrational" explanations of events assume this version of time to be the correct and only one, then we are left with the option that we do not at all have an objective grasp of either history or time and that these abnormative events which interrupt our complacency are, in fact, evidence of this failure of understanding.

I think it is more or less obvious that the assumption of the linearity of time—it passes and does not come again—is very much a historical, and as we have already seen and will see again, a recent construction of a very specific kind of society, one with measurement devices such as clocks, first haltingly used in the late medieval period. At the same time, this concept is objective insofar as it shapes our social reality with mighty hands. Either we are recalling now-distant versions of humanity that lie primordially within our also now very much global experience, or we are desiring that other kinds of time be part of our linear lives, if only for some relief to both the tension that history, including our own, is just "one damn thing after another." The desire to interpret some more enchanted sensibility into the rationalized world of work, schedules, deadlines, and on top of all of this, the nagging anxiety that we face an ultimate deadline in our mortality—and in the meanwhile we may ask just what are we doing to acknowledge that mortality with any profundity rather than merely filling up the interim with ultimately purposeless tasks—likely explains the presence of what appears to be a rift in the normal continuum of time.

If only it could be that we lived as did our ancient ancestors, and the apparent cultural analogs that, in remote regions of the planet today, still exist as radically different human societies with correspondingly different existential outcomes. We can take some solace in the fact that our distant ancestors likely did live in this way, and that their beliefs were as powerful or as weak as our own. They knew not higher truths, but human truths, and we are no different in this regard. The unevaluated return from the pool of souls is a beautiful idea nonetheless, and, as with all understandings of the afterlife, we have no evidence further than our beliefs that it might be at least as correct as the notions that we will explore during the remainder of this book.

That this kind of more or less immediate return to life from death obviates the finality of death is the very reason why it must be characterized as a kind of afterlife in the first place. We must not be led astray by our usual biases that an afterlife must mean some other kind of existence that takes us to another world. This is a very much more recent idea, and there are equally good historical and ethical reasons for its continued presence, perhaps more so than with the others to be explored. That unevaluated return in turn generates the idea of past lives will also be more fully detailed in the next chapter, where a return to this world is also posited, but its nature and character is determined not by the happenstance of birth and death alone and the kinship amongst certain classes of humans and other aspects of the natural world such as animals like snakes or apparently non-sentient events like winds or rivers, but more importantly by an intervening judgement. The mourning of past lives is as much a sorrow for the past life of our cultural history, now that we know for the first time much more about it than did any other age of humanity. The call to return to a time of human consensus and egalitarianism is a call to return to the origins of what we are.

There remains one final note to add. During the writing of this book my wife and I were told that a teenage girl had, some few years before, died tragically in the basement of our home, the very place where many of my books have been written. She hailed from a culture that was a part of the grand fabric of mechanical societies and first nations, and which held beliefs concerning the afterlife and human history very similar to the ones discussed as "unevaluated return." May such beliefs still animate our existence. This chapter is dedicated to her.

3

Types of Belief Regarding the Afterlife

Part 2: Evaluated Return

    A bridge can be made from the concept of unevaluated return to that of a return controlled by a form of judgement about the life just lived. The connection that must be made in order to move from the idea of an unevaluated return to one that has been judged in some way is that the once-interchangeable spirit becomes associated with a specific life or series of lives. This conceptual change occurs in a number of different ways, mainly centered around the sense that the one who is newly dead had some special function or skill that could either be passed on to someone who is just now coming into human life, or could be passed along to one who has already been living and who himself may have a different spirit inhabiting him, although one which apparently is open to the divergent talents of his ancestry. This notion can only develop in societies where there is at least some specialization in the division of labor. Some persons in these cultures indeed do different things, know differently, and have different experiences than their peers. The idea of peer, in fact, becomes defined by a kinship that is more thoroughly human than that found in the so-called "totemic" societies that we discussed in the previous chapter. Now we no longer have beliefs that include a homology between animals or natural forces and human beings. We are not literally snakes anymore, though we may be related to the lions through a fictional apical ancestor, for instance. At the very origin of our family tree, its apex, a union may have taken place during the time of myth, when animals and humans, culture and nature, were not completely distinguished from one another.

This is certainly the case in the region where I am from. The transformer beings had the power to become humans or animals, and perhaps other natural phenomena as well. Some could turn persons into stone—a favorite variation on a broad cross-cultural theme which lasts even into the later agrarian religions, as Lot's wife found out—and when they did, this was (somewhat ironically) seen as a token of their esteem. Stone weathers far better than does human flesh, and thus one could attain a kind of immortality if complimented in this way by the transformer. Once Raven had opened the clamshell and exposed the first peoples to the wider world, there were many encounters between these early humans and the extra-human beings who still were present. One narrative has a man surprising some of the transformational beings performing a dance of transformation. Such a secret could not be passed on to mere humans, so the beings gave the man a song and dance that mimicked this transformation in return for him forgetting about the real thing. Such a story clearly demarcates the line between mortal humanity and immortal extra-humanity, a structural theme that almost every culture known practices or represents through their myths. The song and dance depicting transformation become part of a mythology that can preserve the reality of the early enchanted world while not directly participating in it as some other form of consciousness, something human beings, while alive, could not accomplish. But what about when they are dead?

It is this radical transformation that just might hold the key to the world of spirits in general. If one passes through this world to that other one, would it not make sense that some other abilities might either be incurred or at least exposed by such a passage, and by consorting with such other-worldly beings? Given that in life this or that person performed certain acts with skill and was not involved in other parts of the cultural day-to-day, might not her effects, material and symbolic, hold within them part of the secret to her skills? Might not the spirit, now freed from its earthly vessel, take hold of these items and endow them with some of its newly-revealed power? Given that human beings in life can only give to other humans what they themselves possess as a member of society, might not death bring about the very kind of transformation that the myths relate?

A once-human being becomes something more than human, or at the very least, something different. Durkheim disdained the notion that even religious sentiment suggested that the dead should accrue more powers than they had when alive. Why should death harbor within it an increase in powers, he wondered? Even if we take his point, the idea of difference is enough. This idea—that the dead have different abilities than the living, even though they have also sacrificed their living abilities, as it were—is intimately related with the reality that in more complex societies, different persons know and do different things, even if all of the work of these still small-scale cultures is related to the whole as a functional unit. The division of labor and developing social hierarchy promotes the idea that such social constructions continue in the brief interim of the afterlife—no one wants to tarry with the spirit of a slave, for example, unless the slave had some momentous skill and was captured for that very role, such as an artisan or a great beauty. We shall shortly see how the greatest system of evaluated return, the caste system of the Hindus, assumes this structure as its version of fate. It is only in much more recent agrarian systems, those born out of irrigation monopolies, that we observe our more familiar sense that death is the great leveler, and that the last shall be first.

Two contemporary stories can illustrate the ancient claim that the skills or personal proclivities of the living may be transferred upon death to more persons than the next born. It is well known that in social groups whose regions exhibit endemic and perennial tribal warfare—even into the 1960s in places such as highland New Guinea and the Amazon jungle such was practiced and has even been recorded in ethnographic films—that the body parts, and especially the brains, of the slain opponent might be consumed or worn in order to share in their earthly prowess. No doubt the flaunting of one's military victory was also a purpose of this status rite. Yet the idea that this other person whom you had killed was not only different from oneself—he was from another tribe, after all, and unrelated by kinship bonds—but also different from other members of the opposing tribe in his abilities and social status, is quite revelatory in the history of human consciousness. Although our modern conception of the individual hails only from the Enlightenment of about three centuries ago, this far older idea has within it the source of the notion of personhood.

In our own century, certain of the Tibetan Buddhists practice a ritual that is called the "sky burial." Far up in the Himalayas, monks dismember the corpse and mix it with cereals and sweets of various kinds, then "mulch" the body parts to a finer form. All of this takes place in front of the family of the deceased. Then vultures arrive and eat the fleshy parts of the body, carrying them skyward as they leave. The skeletal remains are then carved into jewelry for family members, to be worn not only as *memento mori,* but as the real organic presence of the spirit that had departed. Although somewhat macabre for our taste, the sky burial ensures that the soul departs from earth not only at its highest physical point relative to where humans can live—the metaphor being that the once-living person has finally shaken off the feet of clay that earthly life has designed for us—but that the living who remain behind on earth are assured that because their kin has flown upwards in the correct manner, they too will be able to follow his fate. He blazes the trail from earth to heaven for them; he precedes their passing and at the same time exemplifies the art of all passage to the other world.

For our purposes, it is more important to note that two things have occurred. One, the bony remains that are now decorating the necks and arms of near relatives speak to an individuation of the spirit, and two, that this individuality, the personhood of the departed, survives death in its character. If a spirit can return, from now on it cannot be entirely interchangeable even with its successive earthly hosts. It must inhabit rather only the kind of person who is alike in a more specific manner to that which had been. It is no longer a category that returns, but an extra-human version of what was once merely human. This spirit is not yet endowed with extra powers, but in fact retains the same kind of powers it had while alive or in human form. This survival of not merely the elemental form of human spirit but its particular personality—as witnessed by the tokens of disjecta membra that now grace by sympathetic magic its cousins—is a crucial movement towards the idea of evaluated return. From now on, the spirit is "aware" that what it has done and how it has acted follows it beyond the earthly stage. It returns with the baggage, as it were, of all of the previous incarnations of its cyclical existence, and thus cannot be said to be just another inhabitant of just another jar of clay. This movement also represents the likely origin of our folktales regarding the represencing of personality traits of the recently dead in the newly alive, as when we say that one's child has his great grandfather's temperament, or what have you.

The Tibetan ritual is at least a couple of thousand years old. But flash forward to an event which occurred about fifteen years ago which, although at first perhaps more morbid than the ritual—after all, in our age we are most of us at least tolerant as slightly naive amateur anthropologists—is fundamentally the same rite. In Norway, an evidently troubled leader of a "Black Metal" rock band decides one morning to thrust the barrel of a shotgun into his mouth and pull the trigger. The loyal and surviving band-mates fashion the shattered bits and pieces of his cranium into necklaces, which they proceed to wear not only at subsequent concerts but routinely as well. Whatever we might wish to say about this genre of pop music in this specific country, and its relationship with criminal acts such as church-burning and even neo-Nazism, the anthropologist would immediately recognize a time-honored rite of sympathetic magic and great respect in the act of decorating the living with the fragments of the dead.

From consuming the brains of defeated warriors in ritual cannibalism to the construction of intimate artifacts from the bones of passed loved ones, there is a sudden recognition that the character of the dead person is not general and not categorical; it is the individuated humanity of the person who was known and loved that is missed. Indeed, it is this more recent style of mourning and memory that exhibits the elements necessary for a belief in a personified return of limited exchangeability. It is but one short step to suggest that the reason for the limits placed on the ability of the spirit to return and animate any living exemplar of a type is due to the specific nature of the spirit's character. This nature can only be developed in life, just as our personal character takes shape as we live on. Just so, its specificity is already judged even before its demise, because one's actions and inactions are befitting only of oneself. We have yet to approach the absolute uniqueness of the individual spirit that is only to be found in very recent Western religions such as Protestantism, but we are now very much on the way to this historical phase.

The pre-judgement that carries its credits and debits into the space of evaluation consists of the life of acts. The question of how one treated others in his society is of the utmost moment. The skills of the deceased as a more specific social role player and laborer in this or that society are seen to be appropriate to a person "of his kind," just as we today—often unfairly—judge someone based on the apparent confluence of ability and work life or social position. The accounting of oneself in the spiritual realm, with a view to returning to this world, is the beginning of the ancient system of particular reincarnation, which overlays historically the yet earlier understanding of general reincarnation. The particularity of this new system is defined solely by the evaluation the spirit undergoes before it is permitted to return and animate some other life-form on earth. Indeed, as the system develops in complexity, the previous categories are blown open, for one might well return in a much lower state of sentience than one had left the previous life with, simply due to the fact that one's previous life did not live up to its potential. The old joke about being reincarnated as a dog or a cockroach was not necessarily a laughing matter. The veneration of the dead and the presumption of sympathetic magic in ritual does not occur in mechanical societies, but only begins to be observed in more complex social organizations that are proto-agricultural, such as those that practice horticultural subsistence. These groups also exhibit for the first time a more complex division of labor and social role, and a nascent social hierarchy that suggests that some persons in society are more important than others. From now on, the weight of past lives gives inertia to that present.

In the radical revolution that displaced transient and nomadic cultures from broad regions north of the equator in Asia and the Middle East, agriculture played a pivotal role. Not only did people settle in one place, using rains and rivers as the fuel for the annual cycle of sowing and reaping, but everything that was human took on an aggrandized scale, far larger and unlike anything that had been seen before. There are two distinct versions of agrarian societies and it is the more ancient guise with which we are here concerned. In India specifically, the division of labor associated with irrigation crop subsistence took the form of not only a social stratification that was markedly hierarchical but also naturalized in its very being: one was born into a category of human being that was considered to be one's proper place in not only the social order, but in the order of nature. This is the caste system, and though it may be familiar to us in its notions of hierarchy and strata of categories associated with certain forms of labor or role, its reliance on a cosmic cycle of evaluated return is foreign to the later agricultural-based social formations of the West. Because of this sensibility, the highest forms of humanity were closer to the gods than they were to the lowest forms of human beings, and indeed, some cultures developed the idea that the rulers were gods on earth, incarnate in human form. One need only think of the pharaohs of ancient Egypt in this regard. At the other end were slaves, or "untouchables," depending on the region—human beings so low on the scale of existence that even to come near them risked being tainted by the magical contagion of whatever deficits their past lives consisted.

We can contrast these kinds of systems with the more recent version of agrarianism that is familiar to any high school history class, that of feudalism. Instead of slaves, there were peasants, and instead of gods on earth, there were human rulers appointed by God through the Church, hence the "divine right of medieval kingship" and the like. It is this later version of agricultural systems that gives rise to the concept of the afterlife discussed in the next chapter, so for now we may leave it be.

In the East and the Middle East, however, there was yet another division that is of interest to us here. Max Weber, arguably the greatest social scientist of all time, and a profound student of religion even though he was not fluent in the ancient languages—Coptic, Sanskrit, Arabic, etc.—that would have made him a strictly religious scholar, simply stated that the origin of the differences between Western and Eastern religions as a whole lay in the distribution of rainfall patterns from east to west. In the east, rain was much more regular, there were far more river valleys, and no large scale empire emanating from one or two city centers could form a monopoly. It was the opposite in the desert sands of the Middle East, where there was little or no rainfall, and but a few great river systems. The earliest civilizations developed along the banks and around the deltas of these places: the Nile, Tigris and Euphrates, the Indus River Harappan culture of western India, and the Yellow and Yangtze in China, to name a few. In western Asia, sedentary culture had sprung quite literally from the dust, hence the mythic narratives of sudden and radical creation with their foreshortened schedules of sometimes but a few days. The process of the growth of cities and urban culture was in the East a much more gradual and diffuse operation. The gods of the East thus were many and had themselves many guises, no more so than in Hinduism. The gods of the West also resided in pantheons, but always there was a supreme god. The religions of the East were also not concerned with their potential competition—their lack of missionary zeal throughout history as compared to that of West consistently underscores this fact—but those of the West made it their official mandate to convert others, or to kill them. Weber said this was simply due to the competition of much scarcer resources in the dryer climes of the Middle East, and the corresponding ability for city states along the few river systems to set up monopolies of force and suasion—only butting heads with other empires when their territorial boundaries met—and of belief systems as well. The gods of Sumeria gave way to those of Babylon and then Assyria and so on, and the gods of Egypt, being ensconced in a more stable set of regimes and cultures, had correspondingly longer vigils over their human worshippers. Yet in India, where there were more gods than any other agricultural civilization but less competition amongst them, the deities' reign and relevance was seemingly eternal.

This is a crucial element in the belief regarding the kind of afterlife under discussion here, that of evaluated return.

If the world of the gods was eternal and diverse, the world of humanity could only be so through the eternal return, not of the same, but of the spirits who were made up of all of the combined differences of their past actions and lives. The accounting of both credit and debit became the sole interface between the two worlds, for the afterlife was still thought of as an interim passage on the way back to the world of human life. We have already seen, however, that the spirit might not return even as a human being in such a system, pending the balance on its ethical ledger.

There were two further developments that acted almost as improvisations on this theme of evaluation. On the one hand, farther east, the cult of the adoration of ancestral spirits became widespread. This "ancestor worship" was ultimately limited to those who were one's direct forebears and through which one could trace not only material inheritance, but one's personal pedigree regarding type and quality of character. At the same time, the ancestors who were responsible not only for your existence but also to a great extent upon your moral proclivities, would dwell in a realm quite close at hand—sometimes seen as being linked to the world of the living by the supernumerary efforts of these self-same live humans to become more spiritual before their deaths occurred, such as by learning specific techniques like "astral traveling" and so on—from which place they would sit in judgement over our progress and regress. Indeed, in older and more traditional Chinese businesses, the ashes of one's ancestors often kept watch from shelves placed above those reserved for merchandise. They were not only watching the fortunes of the business per se, but also over the behaviors of the living who only appeared to preside over their own interests. Thus evaluation in this case worked both ways. The ancestors were adored and supplicated by offerings and prayer, but were also mistrusted insofar as they were imagined to distrust the living. There was always a sense that one's forebears would have done a better job than one's own generation. This kind of demographically oriented judgement is quite familiar to us in the West, as each preceding generation foists its ambivalence about the very existence of its children onto them. Paul Simon's famous lyric, "That was your father, that was your mother, before you was born, dude, when life was great. You are the burden of our generation, I sure do love you, but let's get that straight," speaks with both urgent and poignant sarcasm to the microcosm of each generation's "gap" with its filial relations.

Aside from ancestor worship evolving out of evaluated return, we also see evaluation in the service of continued otherworldly existence, this time farther west of India. The following chapter will detail this form of the afterlife, which will likely be the type most familiar to readers. Here, the judgement comes not from one's human ancestors but from some extra-human being who is the apical ancestor of all humans: a creator God or gods. The idea of having to live up to one's pedigree is here extended in its most radical sense, as we are aware that humans cannot be as the gods are. Like most mortgages, the mortals own the house—the earth as the property of all properties but which, like any property, may deteriorate—and the immortals hold the loan papers. The interest from the borrowing of the credit of existence itself piles up as one lives on, and the debt must be paid with one's very soul. If one defaults, the soul is headed for the oblivion of a dark underworld, but if one makes good in the world and pays regularly on this existential debt, one's soul is offered retirement in a better place.

For now we must return to the source of both these offshoots, the idea of evaluation with a view to a transformative and reincarnative return to the same world that one had only temporarily left. The interim space of judgement occurs rapidly; the ethical ledger has been transacted and accounted for piece by piece, moment by moment. If the ancestors returned to this world to be our judges, their return is presaged by the trend and fashions of the acts we commit prior to their actual deaths. Hence the folklore regarding deathbed confessions, requests, and curses. Before our predecessors leave us, they had best communicate their experience and judgement to us, with at the very least the sense that they will continue to view us in this light if we ourselves do not change in the requested manner. The sensibility that the dead can still evaluate the living is "hypostasized"—made metaphorically cosmic in scale—in cultures where a god or the gods serves as a general vehicle for the judgement of history and fate. The ancestors have contributed to a pedigree that we must now live with. The inertia of history is writ through not merely memory, as we have seen, but also the sense that by virtue of habit, custom, convenience, or practicality, we too will follow in their footsteps. Santayana's often misquoted dictum is testament to this regard, but he immediately adds that just because we have knowledge of history does not mean that we will not indeed repeat it still.

Yet aside from these two evolutionary offshoots of evaluated return there is a third form, unrelated culturally but coming out of similar rainfall-driven irrigation agriculture as in India. This is the form of evaluated return that is played out in the cycle of time and cosmos amongst the grand cultures of Meso-America—the Maya, Olmec, Toltec, and Aztec, for instance. With the Mayan groups in particular, there is the strongest sense that history follows a pattern of eternal return. Indeed, the Maya used the Spanish conquest as evidence for their understanding of time and world, and even as a prop, as when they contrived to get the Spaniards to conquer their final city-state in 1697. The Spanish themselves had not the least interest in risking their small forces against the centre, situated on a well-defended isthmus. Cortez himself had looked in on the city some 170 years before and decided that it was "not worth it." But according to the Mayan calendar, the lifespan of this particular city would come to an end in the year corresponding to the one just mentioned. The actions of the Spaniards was a fortuitous way in which to serve the prophesy. One can only wonder what the Mayans would have come up with had the European conquerors not been around to fulfill their destiny. In the cyclical temporality of agrarian cultures, the return is guaranteed, but evaluation per se is not. Thus evaluation can occur in two ways. One, the other-world can evaluate individual lives and assign them a new place in the system of this world. Two, whole cultures can be evaluated by living up to their cosmic fates again and again. In the second type of evaluated return, the entire society returns to this world in place and as they were, to begin the cycle over again. If they do not perform the narrative of the cosmic cycle correctly, time itself will end. To this day, in rural Mayan communities, the theatrical performances relating to the conquest and the subsequent syncretism of Christianity and pre-Columbian belief systems has the singular theme that time and history must be repeated if they are to continue at all.

Thus evaluation is held here to be active in the broadest sense. We have a resonance of this understanding in our own cultures when, however rhetorically, political leaders or philosophers suggest to us that the future will judge our acts, and that as well the past sits in judgement of us. The future awaits our decision, our children will benefit or suffer accordingly, and history will not forget that though it now moves linearly ahead, it does not thrust bravely into the void without at first and always looping back upon itself for momentary perspective, just as we saw that memory and anticipation our inextricably linked in our own lives.

For the Maya and like cultures, the cyclical view of time and its self-evaluating mechanism of measured performance might involve strange bedfellows, but it does prevent the history of other cultures becoming too much of an imposition on their own. It is well known that when cultures do not have a sense that what is occurring is what needs to occur according to their own cosmology, they are either assimilated or wiped off the face of the earth by more powerful social forces. The survival of the pre-Columbian beliefs and social organization, albeit transformed, is due very much to their ability to negotiate the intrusiveness of strangers and make what is at first alien their own. The calling upon the Spanish to fulfill Mayan prophecy was a brilliant stroke of inspiration, for it not only allowed time to continue in its fated metaphoric sense, but it also allowed the physical culture of these specific Maya to continue without being completely obliterated, which surely would have happened when the Spaniards inevitably got around to finishing the Mayan civilization off. For the Maya, ritual history is a performance in itself, and all theater in this culture is the propitiation of Time. Time is the force even the gods must obey. Time sets its own limits, and the cosmos is measured in terms of their length. In order for themselves as persons to be in the space of the good in itself, Time must be correctly measured, and this is accomplished by the repeated performance of crucial events in the tenure of this or that cycle. To do otherwise is seen as committing evil, for it is an act against the fates. The Greeks had a similar sensibility when they reminded themselves that while there was such a person who contradicted social norms—whom they referred to as a "moron"—the truly dangerous individual was the one who defied the fates. He was called, fittingly, the "hypermoron."

Cosmic limits, whether of fate, time, or mortality affected the personal lives of all concerned within this or that culture. Within the caste system—the archetypical manifestation of evaluated return—the idea of social mobility was nonexistent, or better, inexistent. It was an idea, in other words, that could not be thought in this world, yet nevertheless existed as part of the function of the other-world. The brief passage between the present life, just ended, and the next one, to be begun forthwith, was the space of such evaluation. As we shall shortly see, irrigation monopolies with other-worldly pantheons practiced immediate after-world evaluation, but with a view to continuation in that other world. Not so for irrigation diversities. One was born into a caste and during any specific cycle of serial lives, could not move in any way beyond this. For caste does not refer to a social position based on one's tasks as performed in the division of labor, but rather to an order conferred upon human beings by nature itself. Akin to animal instinct then, caste was part of the very definition of both things and people. The so-called "untouchables" of India were of the lowest form, barely human at all, whose presence was thought to be risky and whose job it was to do the dirtiest of jobs. The risk of caste contagion was, of course, not the same thing we might feel in modern society when we shun the homeless person by crossing the street or ducking into a store at their approach. Contagious magic may work both across social but also natural boundaries, if the society believes that its effect can be "stored up," as it were, and unleashed at some moment inopportune to the person who was unfortunate enough to encounter one of its negative sources. Conversely, if one hung around the Brahmin priests—those at the very opposite of the caste spectrum from the "untouchables"—some of their higher credit may rub off, transporting one upwards in the natural order in the next life. It certainly is ironic to us in the West that the Brahmin traditionally made their subsistence by begging alms. This arrangement manifested a convenient function in two ways: those who gave accrued credit in the karmic cycle, and those who received avoided tasks for which their caste status made them spiritually unfit, thus also avoiding a diminution of the credit they had already accumulated in past lives. Given that the Brahmin were closest to an extra-human presence on earth, they were thus also the reincarnative goal of many in the traditional Hindu caste system. One could eventually ease themselves out of the seemingly endless cycle of serial lives, but there was an ambivalence regarding the benefit of being as a god.

In part, the rise of Buddhism provided a new response to this ancient question of what constituted a better life, and, to follow in the next chapter, so did the idea of ascension in the West. With Buddhism, simply put, one had the choice about whether to move on to a Nirvana or to return to help and teach others about how one attained ultimate enlightenment. Thus evaluation and return were still present, but self-evaluation took equal standing with the natural or cosmic evaluation that placed the person in the position of having to make such a choice in the first place. Ascension without choice proved to be a more finite response in the sense that those "left behind" had to figure the process out for themselves, and indeed, this was eventually seen as the ultimate test of one's faith in these newer systems, such as Christianity, especially in its Protestant versions.

The caste system also generated the preconditions for a type of vindictive resentment with which we are very familiar in modern capitalist society. "Ressentiment," perhaps most easily defined as a kind of malicious existential envy—we resent the very fact that the other, the object of our envy, is even alive at all, and wish him oblivion in spite of also saying to ourselves that his life is not worth living—is rife within any society where the ideals do not match the realities. No society has a greater degree of unfamiliarity between its ideal realm—the shoulds and should nots of our beliefs—and what actually goes on in the world than does our own. If we are equal under the law, or even by philosophical definitions such as those found in the Enlightenment doctrines of universal humanity, yet are very much unequal in the social and material realities of the everyday, ressentiment will be one of the major results.

The German philosopher Max Scheler reminds us of the fable of the fox and the grapes. The fox cannot get at the fruits he knows to be tasty, and so eventually comes to deny that he craves them at all. Furthermore, no animal in its right mind would wish for such "sour grapes." To one steeped in ressentiment, the fruits of life should wither on the vine. Now, this ethical problem by no means attains the level of a progressive structure in such a society. Rather, it aborts or obfuscates ethical action that would ameliorate the problem by turning it into an individuated form of repressed envy. Nothing good can come of it, simply because its "vertical" dimension is drawn on false premises. What is better actually is better, the grapes are not sour, and we do desire them. If we cannot reach them by the usual means, we can either create new means for attaining the same goals—the American sociologist Robert Merton famously refers to these kinds of persons as one of the major sources of innovation in our society—or we can change the goals while not ignoring that the previous goal was still worth attaining by the old standards. We cannot, in other words, deny the existence of the other person just because we do not have what they apparently do, whether talent or wealth or beauty or community. The caste system takes the potentially very strong presence of ressentiment—for who could deny the steep verticality in any system where by nature one is of a lower type than the next person—and places it into the other-world. By leaving the evaluation to the brief passage between serial lives, it allows living human beings to contemplate their next incarnation with a view to improving it and thus shuts down most of the existential envy—a feeling that is certainly a debit in itself, "bad karma," as is said—that the person who finds herself at the short end of the hierarchical stick might well be tempted to act upon. Whatever else the idea of evaluated return implies, it is the idea that one has another chance that is most animating of trying to fulfill one's role in the best way possible. In naturalized systems such as caste, the "best way" means conforming to what is conferred upon one by the immortal powers of the cosmos. After all, the next time around will show that one has "gotten ahead."

We do have one—at first, strange—resonance of the idea of return in our own society. It is odd because on the face of it, we cannot tell whether its possible reality concerns an evaluation or merely a return without any kind of interim judgement. I speak here of course of the idea of "past lives," popular in para-psychological literature as a form of therapy, and well known in the circles of the so-called "new age" spiritualities, those that have combined some altered versions of both Western and Eastern belief systems. Just exactly what constitutes the presence of what are apparently someone else's memories in our life is a bit of a mystery, one that even the pre-eminent scientist and rationalist Carl Sagan considered worth cautiously investigating. What makes such potential cases of serial mortality interesting is precisely that the "someone else" is dead. Sagan stated his interest in these phenomena due to the presence of several cases where young children appeared to have detailed and accurate memories of persons living up to one hundred and fifty years before. These persons had been dead for many decades, even over a century, and records of their lives were known to exist only because they were obscure civil servants in government offices in the same or even in different countries than where the children, our contemporaries, resided. I say "obscure," but of course, one need not travel very far back into history to find that the vast majority of those who lived during that time left no historical record at all. No trace—perhaps other than our almost equally obscure contemporaries' marking of names in a family genealogy—would exist of these persons without bureaucratic records of their assigned and completed tasks. Often the records were in other languages than those spoken by the children in question, or their families. It appeared that the children's "memories" could have come from no known source, and thus pointed in the direction of the idea of past lives. Such documented cases are few, but they do raise an interesting challenge to conventional understandings of both consciousness and time. We will see in Chapter Six that our idea of nothingness is actually rather narrowly defined and concerns our concept of consciousness and not other concepts such as matter and temporality.

The idea of past lives, whether as a fact, therapy, or personal fable, is not native to either mature Western religions or to science. It hails from reaches marginal to our cultural consciousness. The idea of a return comes at least from the great systems that developed reincarnation as the manifestation of some kind of existential evaluation. Yet equally well past lives fit into the even older idea of simple and unevaluated return. We have now discussed both of these ideas, and it is interesting that one final resonance of their presence in human history has resurfaced in a society that celebrates rationalism, often at all costs. It is perhaps amusingly ironic that such cases of past life "memory" can be documented only through the records of a rapidly rationalizing society and through employment in bureaucratic organizations. Yet this should be regarded more as a coincidence, given that such records would at once be plentiful and trivial, both good variables for the survival of documents within the maelstrom of vicissitudes even recent history has exhibited.

The challenge to convention has a further and perhaps more disconcerting aspect. If past lives do occur, and our consciousness has a serial incarnative existence, is it just some of us who return? If so, why? If only a very few cases exist where substantive evidence might be available to document claims of past life memories, have others of us simply forgotten our past lives, have we had any of them at all, do these memories come out in other ways that do not take the shape of usual remembrance, and so on. The cases of children recalling adult memories from other times and places raise a number of interesting and related questions for the rest of us. The problem has been investigated by para-psychological studies, but the persons I have researched in both psychiatry and physics all agree that anyone, given the right kinds of suggestions, and especially under hypnosis, can come up with very detailed and convincing accounts of what seem like past lives. It is a simple and well known fact that our minds create projections when the senses are dimmed either by "trophotropic" phases—like alpha states of consciousness, or the periods between being fully awake and sound asleep—and the construction of past life narratives under hypnosis or other like "therapies" may be deemed part of this category of consciousness, akin to sense deprivation experiments about which the famous Hollywood film *Altered States* philosophized. It seems therefore that investigations other than those strictly archival reach a dead end. We can only speculate about the true nature of such apparent past life memories, as they do not seem to be susceptible to the usual scientific understandings we bring to the study of cognition. Of course, the character of such speculation can tell us much about our own anxieties and aspirations, if nothing else, and thus a sociological study of such "theories" of past lives would be useful.

The idea that consciousness returns to take form anew is an ancient one, predating other ideas that state that consciousness simply continues in another realm, and does not return to the one we know and hold so dear. If fragile truths turn out to be the stuff of serial immortality, if at least some of us do return to live again in the only form of intelligent mind that we are so far aware of, then we may find that the memories which apparently percolate across the divides of time and space are not at all as profound as the wonder that gives them life.

4

Types of Belief Regarding the Afterlife

Part 3: Evaluated Continuity

The form of afterlife discussed in this chapter will likely be the most familiar one for many readers. Instead of returning to this world, whether as civil servant or cockroach, whether evaluated by cosmic forces or simply ignored by them, this idea of the afterlife proposes that consciousness is transformed and continues life in some other world beyond the usual mortal and human ken. "Evaluated continuity" occupies the chronological middle ground in our historical schema, coming after the ideas regarding return and before other notions of the afterlife to be discussed in the next two chapters. Its first major proponents were the ancient Egyptians, and as more recent and more fully "Western" religions descend in large portion from these early beliefs, we will begin with the notion of the underworld, the arena where the evaluation of the soul takes place.

What was a mere interim, a way-station on the passage back to this world, has now become a weigh-station on a freeway that stretches away from the world that we have known to a new destination that is un-thought-of. Or rather, two different destinations, both of which will be unlike anything we have known. This preliminary stop holds within it the place not of judgement per se, but of the data collection that allows an ultimate judgement to then take place. How is this accomplished? What is there to human life that allows it to be compared and contrasted with other life? It is not that we are being compared to other forms of consciousness. No, this is strictly a human affair, though indeed other forms are performing the comparison. Yet even here, it is we who have committed the deeds, thought the thoughts, goaded ourselves to action, or remained passive in the face of the world. The gods are merely accounting for all of these life events in a manner that mortal memory cannot do—often because of the very pride that Nietzsche mentioned had the habit of overturning empirical and objective recollection. We are also not being compared against the lives of others, for this weigh-station is the place where collective sentiments are applied. That is, it is the space of morality. The only question that is relevant here is "Have I lived a moral life?" We answer for ourselves with both our deeds and our beliefs. Though the actual nature of the beliefs of the ancient Egyptians remains somewhat obscure, we can safely say that they, like our more recent cultural ancestors, held strongly to the ideals of a civil and hierarchical order of things within which different kinds of persons performed different roles in order for society to function. Whether slave, priest, scribe, mother, or warrior, each member of such a society could be moral only within the category of a moral order. This is why, when the first manifestation of monotheism saw the light through the declarations and reformations of Akhenaton and his consort, Egyptian society was abruptly turned on its head in a revolutionary manner. It is no surprise that when the pharaoh himself died, Egyptians rapidly restored the old order, destroying Akhenaton's architecture and inscriptions as fast as they could. Nature itself had been upset, even though the Egyptians had always worshipped the sun god, Amun-Re or Ra, whom Akhenaton elevated to the sole relevant god. For that moment, no longer were there gods in a pantheon, but a God, supreme and unhindered by the desires of other beings. Not that it was the desires of other gods that got in the way of an immortal and infinite will, but rather that the pantheon included all kinds of role-players, from Horus to Isis to Anubis to Bas-Tet or Akeru. In other words, the irrigation monopoly pantheons simply mirrored the state of the society they were to rule over, and this is why the social order appeared to be also a natural one. Indeed, one of the most important roles attributed to the god Horus, the falcon god, was the weighing of the life lived in comparison to the gravity of the spirit. This balancing of the scales, the very first such image we have in a lengthy genealogy of the concept of justice, appears often in hieroglyphics and painting. It is very much like the supposedly modern and atheistic idea of "from each according to his abilities, to each according to his needs."

If the life lived did not measure up to the weight of the spirit held within the one who had lived this life, there was a problem. One might well be relegated to remaining in the shadows of the underworld, forever kept apart from loved ones who had passed before oneself. There was a measure of fitting irony to this kind of judgement, as it was also assumed that in life one had kept oneself aloof from the love of others by hoarding one's abilities and talents, or by deliberately not letting them blossom forth. Only the gods could decide whether or not the world or indeed these others themselves had gotten in the way of our proper efflorescence. If the balance was accomplished in whatever manner over the life-course then the soul of the dead person moved on. It was dubious whether one could here speak of any kind of excess, as the surprising perspicacity or dogged determination of those who rise above their lot could always be attributed to the gravity of a spirit which had at first been belied by one's social station. For there was, unlike within the Eastern systems, some kind of social mobility in the societies of the Middle East. Rulers might rise from the ranks of the military or from the cadres of intellectuals or religious figures. A slave might gain his freedom through work or loyal acts of bravery. Strikingly, a woman might become the pharaoh. This kind of movement, rare but known, must have aided in the efforts not only of social control and the out-flow of potential ressentiment, but also produced the ability to dedicate large amounts of labor to massive and unheard-of projects of monumental architecture.

Aside from the usual coercive structures that exist in any large scale agrarian social organization, the very love of the gods must also have inspired the ancient Egyptians, along with perhaps an equal amount of fear. Yet they knew, as we do today, that one's own actions ultimately were the source of the judgement of the gods. Unlike the later Greeks, to whom the gods were sources of both mistrust and whimsy, and to whom the fates were as facts of nature and could not be brooked in any way, the Egyptians took it upon themselves to order their world according to human measures, even though these inevitably became hypostasized as principles descending from the absolute. This is why it is they and not so much the Greeks, who supplied the key and originary elements of Western religion, just as for the same reason it was the Greeks and not the Egyptians—with their seemingly obscure, occult, and superstitious magical rites of embalming which still provide entertainment for Hollywood audiences to this day—who supplied us with the key elements of our sciences.

Yet the question remains, given the inertia of the history of pantheism, many gods performing diverse and discrete functions in a mirror of the new agricultural societies, how did Akhenaton and others who followed him come to dream the idea of a single God, luminescent and infinite? Weber suggests that it was once again a simple function of the environmental metaphor of the source of life. In the East, as we saw, rainfall patterns and copious river systems suggested a pantheism of beings who could not be said to be ultimately superior to one another. This idea in Hinduism apparently came much later, and perhaps even in a response to the revolution of Buddhism, where one path alone became seen as that of enlightenment. But in the Near East, the vast regions of desert suggested something quite different. The source of life and subsistence was both rare and singular. The river systems flooded their respective alluvial plains according to strict seasonal cycles, and only those who lived in this fragile lushness would survive, at least as a sedentary culture. Weber framed these kinds of agrarian organizations as irrigation monopolies, and it was this material reality that eventually gave forth the idea that there might well be only one god, perhaps at first a superior amongst a group of deities, but later appearing as a singularity. Of course it was the ancient Hebrews who went all the way with this idea, and their historical connectedness to still later forms of religious thinking such as Christianity and Islam is well known.

That there is no compelling evidence that the cast-out followers of Akhenaton joined with the then still nomadic Hebrews does not mean there could not have been some kind of resonance to this idea that was both a revolution and a revelation. The Hebrews themselves, caught as they were in the unenviable hinge between two major empires—or rather, between the Egyptians and a whole series of empires emanating from the Tigris-Euphrates region—could not be faulted if they turned their guiding light into a kind of mascot God. This God, for the first time, had a "chosen people," and it was this God that first manifested both a jealousy of other gods, or at least their worship by his people, as well as showed humanity that God himself had a right to resent both the cultural intrusion of others and their respective gods but also was right in eradicating them in order to save his own people. Weber himself, extending Nietzsche's sparse comments to this regard, understands the entire origin of ancient Judaism to be a massive effort in reworked ressentiment. This makes sense if we imagine the Hebrews to be motivated only by the sense that their culture should survive at all costs and that both the Egyptians, who had enslaved them, and the Babylonians and Assyrians, who had co-opted and then attacked them respectively, should perish. This seemingly xenophobic reaction to other cultures is understandable given how the empires treated marginal groups, then as now.

Indeed, it is one of the ongoing ironies of the Middle East that each nation-state is guilty of marginalizing minority ethnic groups within its borders, from Kurds to Sunnis to Palestinians et al, mimicking what we know of the history of the region as far back as writing extends. Given the indefinite origins of monotheism in the potent mixture of self-preservation and ressentiment, it would behoove us to look more closely at the latter concept to see how the entire idea of evaluated continuation took a more enduring form.

The German theologically-inclined philosopher Max Scheler's analysis of ressentiment in light of Nietzsche's re-evaluative pronouncements concerning its presence and its social implications plausibly remains the most detailed but most uneven treatment of the concept. Scheler attempts to rehabilitate the *kerygma,* or elemental and ultimate ethical message of Christian ethics from Nietzsche's apparently all-encompassing critique of it. It is an open question whether or not his attempt is successful. This is so due to the problem of interpretation of the scriptural "sources" of New Testament suggestions and indictments, and the sense that since Nietzsche we cannot truly call this zero-point of a new ethics "Christian," as it ostensibly occurs before Paul and in the light of the Hebrew heritage of the Jesus himself. If we can salvage an ethics free from ressentiment from this very early and at least partly imagined period of the birth of a new set of beliefs, then it would be more historically correct to suggest a different name for it than Christianity. There is no guarantee at the beginning of any investigation into the beginning that such a parsing is merited.

There is also a strong timbre of ressentiment in Scheler's own text—at least the second half of it dating from 1914–15—thereby marking a turn in his analysis toward the rehabilitative and apologetic from the strictly critical. Given that Nietzsche had already covered the bases of the problem of morals, as it were, there is a sense that any other interpreter who carries forward this critique with the hope of new insight does so in the full presence of doubt. "What more can be said?" is a question that haunts more than mere graduate students, and is especially daunting in the field of the humanities and the reflective consciousness of philosophy. Yet Scheler confronts this task boldly.

Why any of this is important to the main course of the afterlife becomes less oblique when one considers the problem of ressentiment in general terms. If one cannot clear a space authentically free from the slavish and vengeful motivation of an oppressed social or philosophical location, then one could only interpret the idea of evaluated continuation, or even judgement in general, in terms of living human beings' sense that things are unfair in this world, so they must be adjusted in or by the other world. Is there something within the boundaries of the religious life that clears it of all need for revenge? Is there something here that antedates resentment? Can religion offer insights about the human condition that cannot be found elsewhere? Yet further, is the religious life viable in any ethical context given our modern situation? (to be described in the next two chapters). Scheler's attempt must be seen in the light of these kinds of questions.

Scheler converted to Catholicism during his work on ressentiment, and so the second half of his text becomes a polemic characterized by the zealotry only new converts tend to exhibit. This includes a cultural over-interpretation of Nietzsche as a great German thinker, against the great European philosopher's own voice in most cases, and this sets up one side of the tension. The conversion experience always, no matter the cultural content, provokes intense hope and reaffirmation of the new faith and enlightenment, and thus provides the other side. In the former we behold the tenor of patriotism and allegiance to "Nietzsche," and the bold effort to further his critique in some way. In the latter we come to know that the way in which to go beyond Nietzsche is to rescue the more or less "Catholic" version of the glad tidings and its concurrent ethics from that self-same critique.

The first portion of Scheler's text is directly loyal to the Nietzschean position, and fleshes it out sociologically. There are many insights here, including the reasonable conclusion that it is our own society that must be most fraught with this slavish moral monomania:

> Feelings of revenge are favored by strong pretensions that remain concealed, or by great pride coupled with an inadequate social position. There follows the important sociological law that this psychological dynamite will spread with the discrepancy between the political, constitutional, or traditional status of a group and its factual power. It is the difference between these two factors which is decisive, and not one of them alone....Ressentiment must therefore be strongest in a society like ours, where approximately equal rights (political and otherwise) or formal social equality, publicly recognized, go hand in hand with wide factual differences in power, property, and education. While each has the "right" to compare himself with everyone else, he cannot do so in fact. Quite independently of the characters of experiences of individuals, a potent charge of ressentiment is here accumulated by the very structure of society (Scheler 2003:28 [1912]).

This kind of obsessive resentment leading to a false evaluation of those who factually have more talent in certain vocations or realms of life, or more status or more power than ourselves, constitutes what Durkheim would call a "social fact." Its character is "larger than life" in that it assumes to become a progenitor of the way in which persons live. More than this, it might be called a mode of being, though an inauthentic one. The study of ressentiment would have to go far beyond its supposed basis in forms of social inequality to expose every one of its exiguous threads. That it is insidious appears certain. Yet it is not only a creeping vice. This form of malicious resentment is said by Scheler to be a character trait of the structure of any social organization that manifests a discrepancy between its ideals and its realities. It is naive to think that even all societies with social hierarchy are guilty of this disjuncture. It is of course plausible that caste systems and ancient agrarian slave-based social forms were "naturally" more free of ressentiment simply because it is imagined that the lower forms of personhood accepted without rancor their naturalized lot in life. We can certainly understand that where there are social forms that are blatantly contradictory in their espousal of ideas of a freedom and equality that remains unmatched on the ground there will indeed be ressentiment.

If sources of such suasion are easy to identify, the management and prudent rehabilitation of the "dynamite" is a more difficult task. Nietzsche suggests in passing that inherited privilege is a strong antidote to ressentiment. If such rights were the lot of everyone we might recreate a society that exudes some more noble sentiment. As such, it would echo in a greatly magnified manner the understanding by Marx's compatriot, Friedrich Engels, of what he somewhat romantically called "primitive communism." The truncated and mislabeled social experiments of the twentieth century aside, we have no clear data as of yet on the function of ressentiment in a theoretically-correct communist society, where private property, wage labour, and the state are consecutively abolished. Given Scheler's insight, one might opine that with the removal of sources of factual inequality and the institution of inherited privilege for all members of a society, a large portion of the sources of malicious resentment would disappear. Aside from these material and political adjustments there would have to be also the socialized sensibility that each person's talents and proclivities would be equally valued and accepted within the social organization. There would also have to be equality of access to skilled mentorship in all fields or vocations. There will always be a human being, let us say, who is both potentially the concert pianist and the pipe-fitter. The religious beliefs of such a culture, if any, would also have to reaffirm the "transcendental" equality of all persons in a more direct manner than those creeds that remind us that "everyone is equal in the eyes of God." Needless to say, such a society is, for now, an ideal.

That it is so can only lend force to the argument that evaluated return is a mere reflection of earthly injustices perpetrated by human beings on one another. It does not help the historical or ethical case that there are still some of us who, upon hearing of some other's apparent vices, immediately and unequivocally state that such a person is "going to hell," or some similar sentiment. In this mode, we are casts as analysts of both a social reality and a worldview that excites and manipulates ressentiment. Scheler further identifies that what becomes a structural social fact within social organization is inevitably "naturalized." The violence this does to the actual source of this emotion is that it becomes both internalized as a psychological constraint and lens, and also that it becomes a "fact of nature" as it were, part of our being human. This in turn allows the marginal person to cast aspersions on whom he imagines is more powerful by "nature." At length, the "criticism" becomes one of this latter's very presence in social life as a person:

> Therefore, existential envy, which is directed at another person's very nature, is the strongest source of ressentiment. It is as if it whispers continually: "I can forgive everything, but not that you are—that you are what you are—that I am not what you are—that I am not you." This strips the opponent of his very existence for this existence as such is felt to be a "pressure," a "reproach," and an unbearable humiliation (ibid:30).

Scheler continues by suggesting that our sentimental biographies of "great men" always document a phase where the higher form attempts to understand and perhaps even love the lower. From "below," this is defined as condescension. As an ethical alternative, we less talented folk must instead simply love another's great works and skills. In general, this is a principle that we can apply to all, great or small. Yet can this ethics of a universal love mitigate the historical inertia of how compassion has been rendered as virtuous in the face of inequality and injustice? Embedded in the now metamorphosed sediment of classical ressentiment we discover bedrock only in the horizon of agrarian civilizations with "natural" castes and categories of human beings, the kinds of societies we discussed in the previous chapter. Whether or not such marginalia accepted the attempted sacred justifications of their lot and of those higher than them is a question we may never be able to answer given that all textual documentation of these periods comes from the social elite, which would almost by definition include those who are literate. Obviously, as an aspect of a general legitimation strategy, such privileged persons and castes would reiterate the social order, if only to reaffirm it to themselves in the light of possible rebellion and ethical qualms. Given this, the ideal situation for a society encompassed with forms of inequality, whether or not formal and legal equality is part of the rhetoric of power and whether or not such is enforced in any degree, is for all persons regardless of status to believe in the impossibility of any other kind of social organization. The American sociologist of religion, Peter Berger, explains:

> It is not enough that the individual look upon the key meanings of the social order as useful, desirable, or right. It is much better (better, that is, in terms of social stability) if he looks upon them as inevitable, as part and parcel of the "nature of things." If that can be achieved, the individual who strays seriously from the socially defined programs can be considered not only a fool or a knave, but a madman. Subjectively, then, serious deviance provokes not only moral guilt but the terror of madness (1967:24).

Put another way, this renders forceful the difference between saying to a child, "That is not allowed," and saying, "That is impossible." The first sets up a normative sanction—precisely the kind of thing that can generate ressentiment—in that it proscribes certain actions or thoughts from emanating from this or that source. Such discriminations appear to know no bounds historically, and those of age, gender, ethnicity, or race are merely some of the most obvious and long-lasting. All children's socialization no matter the culture, and all of our own memories of childhood no matter our backgrounds, are replete with such defeated challenges to the nascent normative worldview into which we are stepping. It is a very different thing, however, to tell someone, young or old, that by nature this or that action or choice is inherently impossible. The one demands obedience from this particular human, the other demands obeisance from the human species. Given this rather contrived division of the cosmos into the allowable and the impossible, it is much easier to understand why Scheler suggests that ressentiment can become "naturalized" as an existential envy. If what, in fact, are socially constructed norms are socialized as if they are intrinsically a part of a nature external to the human condition yet defining it, then the jealous though pious hatred of a higher form of humanity takes on the self-same cosmic import. Laughable, one might be tempted to suggest at this juncture, unless one recalls what ressentiment is capable of accomplishing on both the historical and the personal stages.

Equally vain from a purely sociological point of view would be the ideas that animate the noble type of person in whatever culture. Like the lower man, the higher one assumes as well that such an order is a natural and timeless one—after all, he or she too has been socialized, though from a very different vantage point, in the same cultural milieu that generates the inequality and the comparison in the first place—and that one's "just desserts" do not even enter into the equation. Scheler continues: "The 'noble person' has a completely naive and non-reflective awareness of his own value and fullness of being, an obscure conviction which enriches every conscious moment of his existence as if he were autonomously rooted in the universe" (2003:31[1912]). It is precisely the obscurity of these convictions and not their content that belies their source. For it is within the semi-conscious and often apparently osmotic primary socialization that such beliefs are formed. That they are not questioned and not even open to question is a function of the "legitimated situation." The remarks by the American sociologist, W.I. Thomas, about the veracity of one's beliefs is always relevant, in that once they are accepted as real, all consequences following from this acceptance in fact are empirically and socially real; our actions in the life-world become as social facts. Scheler is hoping that there are primordial elements of essentially religious and thence institutionalized thought that escape both the production of, and the victimization from, ressentiment. Perhaps a clue can be found in the social locations that appear to be the most free of that same problem.

It appears that when avenues for the public discharge of the emotions that generate ressentiment are afforded the general populace, such more malignant tumors are cut off at their source. A list of such earthly arenas, however, tends toward the medieval and morbid-minded, and although no doubt efficacious in some manner, would hardly grace the table of noble repast in our own age. So the locations of political or even routine discharge of hatred, envy, and revenge appear more akin to temporary measures, allowable under the guise of justice while holding dearly and more authentically to that of social control. It is at this precise and problematic point that the conception of evaluated continuation steps in to solve the dilemma.

It does so in three ways. First, it allows those in authority in agrarian society to exact revenge on those who transgress the norms in the name of the other world, which in any case is deemed to be waiting for the souls of the convicted on earth to pass along and be re-tried, as it were, in a higher court. This in turn ameliorates the problem of human error, because if the innocent are found guilty and executed in this world, as they often have been over the course of millennia, then they shall receive the justice due to them in the other world, thus absolving human beings of any lasting responsibility for either immoral action or even death itself. Finally, evaluated continuation means that neither the guilty nor the innocent come back to haunt us in this world. The first are forever damned and sent into the shadows of the underworld, and the second are forever blessed and receive perhaps even over-compensation for their earthly suffering, being attended in an infinite paradise. At one stroke, the brilliance of this new historical development is revealed: no need to worry overmuch about judging people in this life, because ultimately human judgement is finite and capable of error by nature, and because it is so in a cosmos which is created not by human design, it itself stands corrected in the realm of that self-same cosmos. The old adage "to err is human, to forgive divine" reflects this situation. It only remains for living human beings to judge according to their best guess regarding what constitutes a transgression of relevant norms—thou shalts and thou shalt nots, etc.—with the assurance that our errors will eventually and automatically be corrected. Ironically, it is this transfer of responsibility to the other world that contains the first hint of the potential immorality of irresponsibility that will generate the nihilism that states that the afterlife is actually non-existent and so it matters not at all what we do in this life. This final and most recent version of the afterlife will be discussed in Chapter Six, but suffice for now to say that its origins lie in the idea that human beings are not ultimately responsible for their actions, an idea that begins in the cleavage between Egyptian and Hebrew religious beliefs concerning the nature of God and the afterlife.

Not that this shift in locating the source of data for evaluation occurred overnight. It also cannot be said that the ancient Hebrews were alone in casting off the accountancy principle that animated Horus and his shadowy crew. The Greeks, as we have already suggested, were notoriously blasé about such things, and their sensibility that the past was more noble than the present only exacerbated their ability to cast to the winds of fate whatever actions were committed by humans. One lived only one's destiny and nothing more, according to Greek mythology, and the great surviving tragedies of the classical period, none more notable that the Oedipus trilogy, hammered this message home in theater and poetry. So, if you combine the idea that one did only what one could do, with the idea that a higher judge would re-try the judgements of humans, we immediately come to the historical position of understanding evaluated continuation as at once a form of both irresponsibility and revenge. This is the least charitable interpretation one can give it, aside from the sense that such an idea itself is pure delusion, and stems from the critiques thereof which are associated with our contemporary views of agrarian religion. Yet there are plenty of sources of interpretation that, without rationalization, attempt to understand evaluated continuation as something which—precisely because it is a form of human life that is evaluated and nevertheless continues in a very non-human realm—suggested to some of our ancestors that they were incorrect in applying their local moralities and customs to the afterlife or the other world.

Perhaps it is the mystical tradition of Christianity that comes closest to the skepticism of modern rationalism in this regard. One of the mystics' most famous statements is sometimes rendered as "What we know of God, that God is not" can be read in a number of interesting ways. First and foremost is the dual sense of doubt and limitation concerning human knowledge—in that nothing we can imagine is anything like what God is really like—and the sense that if our mortality is known to us and fully present in our lives it is precisely because humanity cannot know the divine. To know God would be to be as Him, which is something mortals cannot achieve. There is even a corresponding doubt as to whether or not the spirit achieves this union in the other world, because even with a good evaluation on its record, the spirit has not been present during all of God's own achievements, including the creation of the cosmos. Thus later Christianity sometimes hedges its bets regarding the status of the spirit in the afterlife as so defined, and this gave forth a multitude of hierarchies of extra-human beings who were not themselves as God—the angels, for instance. Yet there is more to this simple statement than meets the eye.

A second possible interpretation is that what we know of God in this world, as a form of human knowing, tells us that God is not in this world, not present to us. It is not merely that we cannot know

God as he exists in the other world, but that He is also not available to us in this world, because of the nature of our knowledge about the world and the world itself. The manifestations of God the Creator that we see all around us tell us nothing about God insofar as we do not have the capabilities to read the book of nature in its autographed hand. The medieval Christians were well acquainted with what the French historian of ideas, Michel Foucault, called the "prose of the world." The world was a text that could be read. It contained signs and augurs, messages akin to the *kerygma* of the Greeks. Today psychopathology labels such insights, and action derived from them, as "magical thinking," and suggests we need to be cured of it. Certainly, this older form of human consciousness does not participate in our modern dichotomy of rational and irrational. Rather, it is a non-rational form of thought. It does not admit to a difference between the enchantedness of the world as a suite of symbols and signs, and the logic of that self-same world which holds the key to interpreting it correctly. That God cannot be known from the world is not the fault of either God or the world, but is only, for the mystics, a further sign of Man's fallen state. We literally lack the "grace," if you will, to read the divine book of nature as it must be read. Yet to be able to do so would describe us as more than we are. We would, once again, have to become as the Creator to know Creation. To know the cosmos in this non-empirical way is to also know why it exists, something that modern knowledge does not really attempt to address other than through a progressive reduction of cause and effect. We will speak more on this problem in Chapter Six. We have not yet exhausted the mystical definition by negation of God.

A third possible interpretation contains the radical theme of modern knowledge. Consider the stress of the clause in question: "What we know of God, that God is not." We have read it already in two ways. "What we know of God, that God is not"—in other words, we do not and cannot know God with merely human abilities. As well, we have read, "What we know of God, that God is not," in that the manifestation of the Creation is not itself like God or can give any permanent sign of Him to us. Yet we could also read, "What we know of God, that God is not," as that we simply do not know anything about God at all—a common interpretation of the radical negation of the mystical tradition. Finally, and most radically, we might read, "What we know of God, that God is not," as a statement that God does not exist at all! We cannot be sure that this was not part of the possible, though dangerous, meaning of the dictum. Even Thomas

Aquinas, who is best known for his copious summary of all metaphysical knowledge of the time, the *Summa Theologica*—the French modern social philosopher, Georges Bataille, finally answered Aquinas with his *Summa Atheologica* some six hundred years later—admits in his late writings that he suffered a severe anxiety about whether or not all of his work and speculations on the divine might be mere rationalizations, and that either God might not exist or that even if He did, humanity could never know Him, and thus never know either way. This was indeed a terrifying anxiety, one probably worse in those days than in our own, more skeptical age.

The concept of evaluated continuation could not by definition respond to such a problem, because of the simple lack of return of the souls to this world. If souls could return, as in previous systems of belief, then we might have some evidence that not only does an afterlife exist but that it actually functions properly, and that some extra-human force is at work in the cosmos. Well, one does have to wait a while for the historical response that did occur, the response that eventually became the modern sciences. There is a force greater than ourselves at work, suggests modern thinking, but it is one that is physical and not metaphysical. At first, this seemingly revolutionary step included its own version of the afterlife, to be discussed presently in the next chapter. Yet this idea itself did not last long. In fact, in spite of the weight of scientific knowledge in the modern, technology-driven world, most people from every culture hold closely to ideas of the afterlife that had their genesis during the agrarian periods. There are some very good reasons for this, even if the inveterate rationalist would greet the consequences of such beliefs with disdain.

The first thing we would wish to know about our sense of evaluated continuation today is not about who holds it as a belief, but rather, and perhaps paradoxically, about those who do not. We know first of all that they are in a small minority. Why so, given the rationalization of the world and everything in it? This ascent of forms of rationality may be the very key to the reason why only a few have adopted the "rational" as the best form of human consciousness. Perhaps the most fitting and amusing version of our reaction to rationalization in social institutions would be the Confucian characterization of Hell. In this underworld, it is the bureaucrats themselves and those who support them who suffer various indignities. The "insolence of officials," as Hamlet's soliloquy aptly puts it, is rewarded its just desserts. In general, however, the idea of a penitential underworld from which there is no grace nor egress appears on the scene when social hierarchies attempt to exert control over illiterate populations. This is still somewhat the case today; the numbers of people who believe in Hell are far fewer than those who believe in God. The idea of godhead and the underworld are not in any convenient or consistent historical correlation. The idea of the New Testament's loving and forgiving God, as opposed to Yahweh, the jealous and vengeful deity, is in part responsible both for the decline in belief regarding divine retribution but also for the decline in the belief in the concept of evil itself, whether of extra-human manufacture or our own proclivities, plentifully exemplified over the course of the last century. Thus evaluated continuation tends to turn out with an "all's well that ends well" kind of denouement. Our sins are forgiven, or we were unaware that we had committed them, or some of what we thought were sins actually were not, and so on. This optimistic view of death and resurrection, the "glad tidings" or "good news" version of mortality, has an immediate appeal, and not merely for those who have suffered at the hands of bureaucracies. If one cannot live as a human being without faith, then it could be considered a bonus of having faith in life and even in the afterlife that one also has, most of the time, hope. Yet hope is not a universally available sentiment, given our world situation, and plenty of our fellow humans live on without it. Hope was also seen as an evil by the Greeks, who thought it led to a false estimation of the worth and purpose of human life, while also providing an illusory relationship with the fates. Hence when Pandora opened the box of elemental aspects of consciousness—one of many versions of the myth of the covenant and its "ark"—she ironically closed it upon Hope, which remained to humans as their only possession in the face of the void. All other abilities had fled heavenward, where they must remain.

The metastasized metaphor of both joy and sorrow generates the dual conception of heaven and hell. We understand both to be universal properties of the human condition, and so why should they not continue in some purified form in the other world, where all aspects of humanity are reduced to their constituent elements? If we have lived up to the gravity of our spirit, if we have ordered our existence in the finite as the cosmos has ordered the infinite, then we have made our lives worth dying for.

5

Types of Belief Regarding the Afterlife

Part 4: Unevaluated Continuity

It was not the scientific and philosophical Enlightenment that attempted to quash belief in the conception of evaluated continuity or continuation, but rather the reaction to these new and radical intellectual movements: the "Romantic" movement, so-called due to its somewhat sentimental sense that life could not be reduced to a mere physicality. Yet it was human life that was the ultimate measure of its own spirit—kind of like the Renaissance idea of "Man" being the measure of all things—and thus it was to human life and it alone that we should look for spiritual inspiration. Hence the position was developed that within the arts of life there was an artfulness of being that guaranteed both the spiritual character of humanity but also suggested that humans could access other worlds of being that coexisted with our own. The Romantic reaction to the Enlightenment thus engendered a multitude of new beliefs ranging from Paley's "natural theology" and later "scientific religion" movements, including the well-known Christian Science that incurred Mark Twain's satirical wrath, to the fetishes regarding ghosts and spiritualism, mesmerism, and most recently, interdimensionality and alternate realities. These last straddle the uneasy divide between physical science as a descriptive cosmology and cosmology itself as a theory of being, or an ontology.

The key element that links all of these disparate beliefs together is the same as what distinguishes them from the categories of beliefs that occurred previously in our history. This is the idea that while consciousness does continue, human life is not the only nor the final form of consciousness, and lives do not necessarily undergo an evaluation and thence a sorting out of souls based on the data gleaned from such a judgement. Rather, there is either a sense of utter forgiveness for even the very existence of consciousness, or there is no evaluation at all. It is this latter idea that gives us the fourth and final version of the afterlife, and completes its four-square model in which consciousness itself can indefinitely reside and where there is posited an afterlife.

The idea of unevaluated continuance raises a new moral problem for society and individual human beings alike. This puzzle is related to that of "theodicy," or the problem of the perfect creator and imperfect creation. For the agrarians, this was resolved in the main by suggesting that the creator gave human beings freedom of the will, exemplified in the Western mythic narrative of the expulsion from paradise. From the leisure and non-responsibility of the garden—a metaphor for the mechanical societies with which we began our investigation—to the toilsome travail of agriculture (the "work or die" ethic begins here), Man's use of his will becomes the source of the tension or divide between the being of the Creator and His creation. The world in itself is perfect, as is the cosmic order, but there walks on its stage another kind of intelligence—lesser, certainly, and mortal. This limited or even truncated consciousness is in direct contrast to that of God's, which is seen as being both infinite and immortal. It is Man himself who is the imperfect creature, and as he is the only other kind of being in the cosmos that combines the native wit of reflective consciousness with the sometimes severe limitations of both his empirical senses and his ethical sensibilities, the problem of theodicy arises only with human beings' willful decision-making in the face of the divine order of things. The idea that such a will is nonetheless God-given complicates matters only in the sense that life becomes a test of both will and faith. Sometimes these harmonize in the mortal version of godhead, but often they are in conflict. The Book of Job in Western mythology is perhaps the clearest statement of this problem, with the addition that the order of divinity so represented is so stentorian in its demands on the faithful that these latter must utterly give over their will in the face of what is deemed to be not only natural, but righteous.

So the new problem that emanates from the one of theodicy simply stems from there no longer being either an evaluation of one's living consciousness as it has lived—no threat of expulsion from a better place to a worse one—or a final judgement that distinguishes those fit for the best place and those who have earned placement in the worst.

Rather, consciousness simply moves on to another form—and there are, as we shall see, a number of competing claims regarding exactly what kind of form this continuation takes—and once the transmigration occurs, new worlds open up to us that are the likeness of those previous only in the sense that they too contain no source of moral evaluation. This problem of the lack of external evaluation places the burden of ethical self-proof directly on humanity. It is the nation-state with its legal apparatus that has taken up the call declared by unevaluated continuation. So much so that the state has the right, indeed the obligation, in certain systems of justice, to execute its own citizens on behalf of yet other citizens who have been legally wronged. The state thus becomes the contemporary form of godhead, and its judgement is the final one. Whatever our individual scruples may be regarding capital punishment, it is clear that disagreement over its morality is produced by the fact that the state kills in its own name, just as did the gods of the previous moral epoch. The nation-state does not invoke a god, for that would make its power a mere surrogate of something higher than itself. If the state ventured back into this relationship, associated with the kind of society in which there was no clear separation from politics and religion or their surrogates, the church and state, then it would leave itself open to conflicting claims regarding just exactly who had the superior morality. In other words, no modern country can afford to let its own citizens question its ultimate use of force, even if this force is directed against those it is presumed to have the obligation of protecting in an ultimate way, either by the removal of those internal to it that constitute a threat to its social order, or by the defense of its national borders, and less immediately righteous, its international interests.

None of this ever occurred as problematic to mechanical societies, the original and yet most recent version of human organization that based itself upon the idea of the lack of evaluation, in that case as we saw above, unevaluated return. This was simply due to the fact that in these tiny human groups, there could be no value conflict and thus no need for an intercessionary system of judgement that today we call the law. As we saw in Chapter Two, the "flatness" of these societies is reflected in the correspondingly horizontal character of their ideas regarding both the soul and its afterlife. Souls were interchangeable across time and space and nothing they could do would distinguish themselves in any metaphysical manner. They were portable and reappeared as the *modus vivendi* for the newly born, after having passed from their previous vessels, the recently dead. They were not evaluated in any way, other than when present within this world they took on the aspects of the culture in which they were ensconced, and acted accordingly.

Acting according to the norms in any society is the primary means by which we self-evaluate. Not only are we subject to the social facts of the day, either fashion or structure, but we also police ourselves. This may take the form of merely doing what we are told until we can get away with not doing so—a tandem of attitudes that is found within every one of us to a certain extent—but it may also rise to the level of an ethics. This reflective and yet critical understanding of our place in society, and our society's place in the larger world of diverse cultures, allows us to question both the veracity and the purpose of our norms. We, in a word, take the evaluative character of what was for the previous age the sole or at least ultimate purview of the afterlife—evaluated continuation—and place it into this world, the one we live in during life. Instead of waiting on the pronouncement of a credit-debit system, whether induced by the structure of the cosmos itself (as in traditional India) or having its division of spiritual labor delegated to the underworld (as in ancient Egypt) or yet hearing it from the fates (ancient Greece), modern society pronounces its own judgements both on individual humans and on itself. The upshot of this is that over the short term, the notion that the other world takes precedence in its evaluation of spirits or souls begins to fade. Indeed, it takes but one glance around our contemporary society to note— either with satisfaction or chagrin, depending on one's values—that almost all of us are much more concerned about the figures we cut in life, and hardly give a thought at all to what we might look like to some other set of forces or beings that hail from a non-human realm and use extra-human measures of existential worth in their accounting processes.

Sagan provides a modern rendition of this schism between "man the measure" and some other form of judgement when he asks us that we consider how we might look to a hypothetical alien species visiting the Earth for the first time. By definition, an extraterrestrial consciousness would have no human concern or value, and would look at us perhaps not objectively, but from a very different viewpoint. He chides us for our lack of "stewardship" regarding the fate of the Earth and its eco-systems, and for our continuing internecine conflicts. Our maturity as a species would be called into immediate question, says Sagan, by the evidence of the empirical events, such events that any species, no matter how different or advanced, could not fail to notice.

Though couched in the terms of a future-looking science, the ethics of this critique are clearly borrowed from a previous metaphysic. The alien species are in the place of God, and the degraded nature is that self-same nature extant outside the Garden after the fall of Man. The judgement is very much the same, fraught with disappointment concerning our failure not only to create a sustainable biosphere and our utter disregard for other species on Earth, but also, and most tellingly, our inability to create a single world that participates in what I have referred to elsewhere as the "envelope of being," given the relationship all human beings have, in their mortality, to the cosmos.

If mechanical societies are deemed to have been in the "correct" relationship with the surrounding nature and also with their beliefs, it is surely due more to the anthropological facts of their parochial existence and the levels of both their population loads and their extractive or manipulative technologies. It is likely pure romance to suggest that earlier human social organizations were "by nature" more aware of their "spiritual connection to the earth," or some such other popular conception of traditional and non-Western societies. Whatever we may have to learn from the few remaining examples of quasi-mechanical societies that exist in the world today, we cannot afford to linger on the notions—of such interest in the eighteenth century—that we can somehow return to, or mimic, these social organizations and thus achieve their material and spiritual effects. Rather, we must look to our own society for answers to the questions it has posed.

There are a number of candidates or categories of phenomena that human beings experience in the modern world that are claimed to be universal in complex social organizations. Through this universalist claim it is posited that their existence might be a sign of the existence of another world. Such a world would be both counter to our own but also juxtaposed with it. It also would imply the existence of extra-human forces or forms of consciousness that might be associated with that world. We will see in the Epilogue that the specifically modern claim that our world is ultimately disenchanted allows for both our explorations of new forms of consciousness, and our aspiration to either create or encounter such forms that are deemed superior to our own. The search for human origins as recounted by the sciences of both cosmology and hominid archaeology is the ongoing attempt to replace the loss of the previous cosmogony, or origin myth, that accounted for the presence and purpose of human beings in the universe. After the intellectual revolution of the Enlightenment, the economic and technological shift of the Industrial Revolution, and the radicalism of the political revolutions in Europe and America, this older cosmogony lost much of its appeal. Everything was, shall we say, reborn; everything was new, including our conception of ourselves as human beings. Given this, we found that it was incumbent upon ourselves not to simply retell the narratives of our ancestors, but to create quite different ones, but with the same ultimate goals in mind.

The questions that the sciences ask are almost the same as those responded to by the great world religions: where did we come from, why (or how) are we here, what are the meanings of human life, what does the future hold for us, etc. Science has of late taken over much of the sacred sphere. Its images are of wonders unimagined on Earth; it tells us of other worlds and perhaps foretells the presence of other forms of being. The territory of scientific explanation has impinged upon that previously held in the suasion of religion, but science does not attempt to answer ultimate questions with the same ease as did the religions. There are a number of reasons for this, but they hold to a specific pattern, and one that may be elucidated from precisely the kinds of "signs" just mentioned, which supposedly hold in their occluded presence not so much the limits of reason—they are not to be understood as irrational phenomena—but the limits of contemporary and paradigmatic scientific knowledge. That is, they still participate in "non-rationality."

We have already seen that the agrarian mind regarded the world as an autographed text, signed by the hand of God or the gods, and holding in it the meaning as well as the method of creation. One could divine the divine, if you will, by studying this text closely and learning its language. We could only but approximate its infinite meaning and purpose because of our finite consciousness, but nevertheless, it lay there close at hand, side by side with our own limited being. The modern take on the meaning of the world is much more strictly reductivist. Indeed, the question of meaning has receded so far from most scientific and rationalistic horizons that it could be said to participate in the production of the general alienation that human beings are said to feel about living in contemporary society. That life is "meaningless" presupposes that the world has no meaning. Physical existence through the autonomic processes of cosmic and organismic evolution are not enough by themselves to generate meaning. Of course, in this locale of the cosmos, it is human beings themselves who must fulfill this task. We cannot expect the world by itself to have provided anything other than our existence, though fragile and threatened, and we often fall short of providing meaning and purpose for ourselves. This is the real problem, the modern mindset says, and not the loss of enchantedness that had its source in some other order of purposeful being. It is this shift in both the location of the source of meaning and the space of evaluation that marks, perhaps as much as any of the revolutions just mentioned, the beginning of our modern world, and remarks upon us as modern human beings living in it.

Berger suggests that we look to the human condition for what he refers to as "signals of transcendence" (1970:52). That is, there are manifest in the everyday world of human life in all of its cultural forms aspects of our character that appear to be primordial and immediate to us. It is these kinds of events, presupposed by the reactions we have to the world around us, that may be signs that the other world not only exists but that our consciousness is connected to it. It is of interest to us here that Berger never claims that the other, hypothetical world being pointed to by these "signals" holds within it an evaluatory function. He does claim that our experience of the death of others is part of an ongoingness, a life experience that attests to the end of the other's presence in our world This is not necessarily to say that the end of the other as a form of consciousness is also for them the end of the world. He presents five aspects of humanness that suggest the presence of this other world.

The first attribute has to do with our predisposition for order. This is "grounded in a faith or trust that, ultimately, reality is 'in order,' 'all right,' 'as it should be.' Needless to say, there is no empirical method by which this faith can be tested. To assert it is itself an act of faith. But it is possible to proceed from the faith that is rooted in experience, to the act of faith that transcends the empirical sphere, a procedure that could be called the argument from ordering" (ibid:54). All cultures certainly impose a human order on the world and on the universe, but in fact there is also a mathematical and physical order to the cosmos that can be empirically verified, so Berger's original point is unclear. This higher order in no way implies any other world but the one we observe, and there is absolutely no necessity that order itself has anything to do with human beings' presence in that order. Even more importantly, there is no evidence that the presence of a nonhuman objective order implies that there should be an extension of being into some other world. This is a crucial insight, as it grounds the content of the next chapter in another kind of faith, that associated with the reduction and ultimate loss of consciousness to a form that indeed is still real and continues, but cannot represent anything sentient as such, let alone human. So the presence of both a human and a cosmic order in our lives in no way presages the immanence of another world where there is also order, or, order which is but an extension of the ones in which we already participate.

Berger's second suggestion is called the argument from play: "Play always constructs an enclave within the 'serious' world of everyday social life, and an enclave within the latter's chronology as well" (ibid:58). Play creates a time out of time and a place out of place, and it does not, contrary to Berger, distinguish between sorrow and joy unless it is to divide their dual presence in the history of humanity amongst actors in a play, where the sadist is enjoying himself and so is the masochist. Yet we might well agree that "Joy is play's intention. When this intention is actually realized, in joyful play, the time structure of the playful universe takes on a very specific quality—namely, it becomes eternity" (ibid:58, italics the text's). Berger also suggests that play is a reiteration of childhood, which as yet has no consciousness of death, and thus suspends our disbelief in our own mortality. That is, rather than reminding us that the everyday world lunges inexorably onward toward a sudden death which is in its essence unpredictable at the individual level, play liberates us from reality by positing another world, which Berger then takes as a sign, in its universality of human feeling and aptitude, that this other world contains nothing but the eternity of joy. Unless joy itself is authentic only in the joy of the other—and even in this, the problem of the masochist remains—Berger's second point falls short of its goal. Play may equally and more practically be seen as an evolutionary expression of a basic, primate instinct of curiosity and creativity essential for the survival of the species. At the same time, play could be considered quite dangerous, as both of these basic and noble human traits have also led us to the brink of total self-destruction. In no way does the presence of play suggest any ultimate or eternal joy emanating from some other world into which consciousness continues, but at the very least it does suggest that we are capable of extending our notion of play into realms hitherto unknown in the "serious" world, and as such we depart from its seriousness in a manner that has no ulterior motive.

Berger's third signal of transcendence is the argument from hope: "Human existence is always oriented toward the future. Man exists by constantly extending his being into the future, both by his consciousness and in his activity. Put differently, man realizes himself in projects. An essential dimension of this 'futurity' of man is hope. It is through hope that men overcome the difficulties in any here and now.

And it is through hope that men find meaning in the face of extreme suffering" (ibid:61). We have already had occasion to remark on the cultural interpretations that the concept of hope undergoes. It is not in fact a human universal, and even when it is present in our consciousness, it appears in a variety of forms, not at all of them salutary to the idea of the future. Hope, for the Greeks, was an evil because it could only prolong the illusion of a future, one that ultimately did not exist for mortal creatures. Even if "the only death we can experience...is the death of others; our own death can never be part of our experience, and it eludes even our imagination" (ibid:62). It is not hope but life itself that pushes us onward in the face of death. Besides, we do not experience the death of the other, as Sartre suggested, but only their dying. And in this we are not limited to the observation of the external world. We also experience our own dying, though not our deaths. By definition, death itself is not something that can be experienced by human beings, and hence the existence of the discourse on death and nothingness that fills the pages of the next chapter below. "Life goes on," we say, either with a sorrowful but liberating wisdom, or with rancor and the animate version of the *risus sardonicus*, the death's head grin.

So much for hope. No doubt it is essential for the continuation of human life, but this is precisely so because the end of that life ends without hope of its further continuation. Of course, those who remain behind nurse that hope, both for themselves and the others newly departed, but this only means that within hope there is but more hope, and not a shred of the reality that one might hope for. Besides this, we are told to be careful of what we hope for, as wish and desire are no more fully cognizant of the future than is any human venture or belief.

Berger moves directly on to what he characterizes as the "argument from damnation." He refers to experiences in which "our sense of what is humanly permissible is so fundamentally outraged that the only adequate response to the offense as well as to the offender seems to be a curse of supernatural dimensions" (ibid:65). Here the word "seems" is the important word. In fact, and especially with the passage of time, all human deeds fade from both mortal and cultural memory. This is indeed one of the most dangerous facts of human existence, but it is a fact nonetheless. What do we know of the terrors of Genghis Khan, or the individuated nightmares of Caligula? That we know something of them at all may well be testament to their ferocity and their evil, but our tolerance for such atrocities has diminished over the centuries, and we are more shocked by what our own history tells us now than we have ever been before. At least, this is also what our history tells us, and we can know no more than this. That we have extended the dimensions of "man's inhumanity to man" in the last century to epic and grotesque proportions, the basic idea behind murder and mayhem has remained the same: if some other individual or group opposes your aspirations, the most convenient thing to do with them in the long run is to kill them off.

In spite of Berger's impassioned but romantic cries regarding the "impossibility" or unimaginability of such acts as the systematic and large scale murder in the Holocaust or even the individual murder of specific children in crimes of all kinds, the fact remains that such things are not only possible and imaginable from the brute physical point of view—to which Berger admits—but that they are historical in their construction. By this I mean that the horrors of the Holocaust were engineered by human beings like ourselves, socialized in a specific environment by other specific people who held specific though despicable views. None of this is out of the ordinary in the sense that socialization of all kinds takes place in a similar manner. People can be trained to do whatever is necessary to aid the survival and reproduction of whatever belief is relevant to them. Killing and dying are only the most extreme forms of this normative spectrum of human action simply because in doing either, one or the other of us is no longer capable of such action, and the future has been abruptly altered, or yet ended by one specific act. None of this is a sign that there is transcendent "evil" in the cosmos, but only that human beings can exhort in themselves an evil whose potential manifest vice resides within most of us. I say only most, because there is also no evidence that what we today call evil was practiced by mechanical societies. Death was a function either of old age or disease, or of the simple defense of one's kin group, something that even our modern law tells us is permissible in certain circumstances.

"Evil" insofar as it exists in the human imagination, is itself presaged on the notion that the good life excludes suffering which is "unnatural." This in turn suggest that such suffering is contrived on the part of others and inflicted unnecessarily on ourselves or others who have done nothing to "deserve" it. All of these moments in the career of evil both nascent and fully formed involve value judgements. If the Nazis insist that the presence of Jews in the world will eventually lead to the world's destruction, we can only point to the massive evidence to the contrary, but we cannot dissuade them of their beliefs. The practice of evil on behalf of Nazi beliefs was ended only with the death of the practitioners themselves, and there seems to be no other way around this historical fact that is in fact more than historical, but existential. That is, if someone holds a belief and needs to kill you for it, generally no amount of persuading will allow your life to continue. One of the problems of human evil is that it also tends to insist that those who oppose it practice some form of it themselves, as when the Allied destruction of German cities and their populations aided their ultimate victory over the Third Reich. Perhaps such carnage of civilians was not necessary, but it was believed to be so, just as there is much evidence that the Holocaust sapped German resources so much that it led to their defeat. If the Nazis and their imagined nemeses had worked together—a thought which is also seemingly unimaginable, as the very nature of Nazism would have had to change, or at least find another easy but external scapegoat, the Slavs, for instance—it is quite plausible that the Third Reich might still be in existence today. Perish the thought, but it only demonstrates that evil is a relative and wholly human thing. One man's saint is another man's fool, and one man's demon is another's savior.

So far we have had no luck in agreeing with Berger's suggested list of transcendental aspects of the human character. His fifth and final argument is that from humor, but here again, the presence of the incongruous and the comic discrepancies of humor of all stripes, from irony and satire to vaudevillian slapstick, only goes to show that, like play, this universal human trait is present as part of our cultural evolutionary toolbox. Humor, like hope, allows us to go on living the morrow, until others can replace us in the great chain of historical being that animates our living immortality. One simply cannot take seriously the value judgement contained in Berger's idea that humor is indicative of the "worldly imprisonment of the human spirit" (ibid:70). The world is not in itself either humorless or comedic. Tragedy and comedy are of human invention and thus also of human import. No animal feels these liberations or these pauses the way we do. Although other forms of consciousness on earth may feel suffering, it is impossible for us to not personalize their anguish unto our own. It is we who feel sorry for the animals, and so we should given that it is also we who have caused all of their unnecessary—dare we say evil—suffering in the world. But for themselves, in themselves, animals suffer pain in their own way, a way in which we cannot share without the imposition of our own bad conscience and self-reproach. Berger wishes us to agree that "humor not only recognizes the comic discrepancy in the human condition, it also relativizes it, and thereby suggests that the tragic perspective on the discrepancies of the human condition can also be relativized. At least for the duration of the comic perception, the tragedy of man is bracketed. By laughing at the imprisonment of the human spirit, humor implies that this imprisonment is not final but will be overcome" (ibid:70). This kind of statement not only assumes that there is a human spirit which seeks its freedom elsewhere than in this world—an idea which is both ethically irresponsible and practically unresponsive to the reality of the world and indeed could be seen as one of the sources of the very tragedy Berger is attempting to annul—but that liberation from the world by some other world is the only remedy for this tragedy. But the real tragedy lies in the belief that this world is damned and nothing humanity can ever do can save it from its own state of damnation.

This idea of humor contradicts Berger's aspirations for both play and hope, and in this also underscores the historical fact that, while humor may have been a temporary antidote for the suffering of our agrarian ancestors who put their faith in a deterministic fate, for modern persons humor is in fact a vindication that not only can we laugh at ourselves, but even at our own history. In this we overcome it, and this overcoming takes place in this world without reference to some other realm where humor in fact would not be present at all, precisely because there would be no tragedy worthy of it.

If Berger does not help us establish with any veracity the existence or the character of some other world, his work and that of many others does remind us that we are living in the age of belief in the kind of afterlife that we have characterized as unevaluated continuation. The goal of these kinds of discussions is to represent to us the idea that consciousness continues, and although it is a very Protestant thing to look for "signs" of our further and future election to another kind of being and another form of world, it cannot be said to appeal to any general human sensibility regarding the nature of the human condition. But another much more famous and philosophically reflective attempt has been made, and no discussion of this last form of the afterlife would be complete without at least a glance at it. This discussion is contained within William James's great work, *The Varieties of Religious Experience*. Originally published in 1902, James—the American pragmatist philosopher and founder of American psychology—provides what he terms a theory of "human nature." Aside from the scientific strides made by this study, the key contribution to an understanding of human desire and imagination that turns toward the ideal and at first away from the real is that what religion is in itself is something that is personal and subjective. In other words, religion is not to be thought of as a history of great ideas or as a series of institutions or social movements. The actual experience of real people is first and foremost in James's account, and it is from these experiences that he constructs the architecture of a fundamental aspect of human nature.

The sensibility of the religious attitude is not at first religious. The idea of vision inspired by the beyond, or by the other world—which now takes on the generalized cast of an infinite repository of abnormative experiences—is something more elemental than any categorical, formal, or indeed, normative interpretation thereof. These interpretations, however necessary to the comprehension, understanding, and communication of these visions (How else does one tell of what the other has not experienced?) are not in themselves what places us at a parallax to the regular reality of everyday social relations. For James, such experiences do not hold our ultimate scientific interest because of their subsequent interpretations, but because their reality points to a kind of consciousness which differs from that of the mundane sphere. It points to the idea of the other world—whether such a world is sacred or merely present, external to us or part of our complex and ill-understood consciousness, is not really at issue. Only by the end of the massive study does James himself begin to point out that religion has been more of an interpretive curtain, acting as a veil on parts of human nature that remain relatively untouched by science, and are separated from our normal waking lives by the "filmiest of screens." At the same time, James's work went very far to salvage the religious life and its attendant experiences from the new psychology of which he was a founder.

The nineteenth century progressively pathologized religious experience as part of its reaction to the ancient régime of theocratic politics and metaphysics. So thoroughly did this scientific and clinical apparatus take over the study of mind and behavior that today we are apt to regard someone who begins to speak of his experiences of God or angels as suffering from some kind of mental delusion, especially if that someone is a stranger to us. Certainly it is more convenient, in the realm of the everyday, to dismiss such people as "crazy" or at least irrelevant, because it allows us to get on with the quotidian tasks of life without engaging in any serious ethical or metaphysical discussions regarding our existence and our actions. Not that every "Jesus freak" is necessarily a serious thinker, but he is someone who has latched on to something that James states is an integral part of every human being: the ability to imagine another world than our own and thus to call our own into question.

This is so because of all of the abnormative experiences we encounter over the life course, some of us begin to pay rapt attention to not only their occurrence, but to their supposed meaningfulness for their lives. And not only their lives, as we well know, for in the West one of the key elements of latter-day religions—Christianity and Islam, for instance—is the necessity for the conversion of the world around them. The saving of souls is seen as an ethical *jihad*, although history shows us that such an excuse can be made for the most grotesque violence and oppression. James flatly rejects the relevance of the vision had by the one for any other person. But for that one, he just as strongly notes that it is imperative that he pays some kind of heed to it, even if the subsequent interpretations and analysis end up recommending to the subject himself that he also should dismiss it as ultimately unimportant. We will see in the following chapter how other kinds of objects in the world which are deemed sacred can then point to the sacred as both an ideal and as an alternate reality, but it suffices for now to understand that James wishes us to take seriously the aspects of our psyche which appear to impinge on our daily life as if from elsewhere: "It is as if there were in the human consciousness a sense of reality, a feeling of objective presence, a perception of what we may call 'something there,' more deep and more general than any of the special and particular 'senses' by which the current psychology supposes existent realities to be originally revealed" (James 1907:58 [1902] italics the text's).

Of greatest interest is that this feeling of presence is not generally part of either our sensory apprehension of the world nor is it something we expect of the world. For how could the scientific understanding of the cosmos be complete if there were some other kind of experience to be understood, one which—rather than leaving itself open to, as James's new psychology was supposed to do—closes itself off from all investigation or relegates such reports of these subjective experiences to the realm of sickness and insanity? The agrarian metaphysics responded fully to such experiences, and when the local fashion of religion did not do so, new religious ideas and even social movements were born because of them. The dual metaphysics of a scientific and aesthetic modernity, which perhaps paradoxically has issued forth both the romantic idea of unevaluated continuation as well as the abyssal horizon of reductive nothingness with regard to the afterlife, takes account of such experiences as part of human life and imagination only. Yet "so far as religious conceptions were able to touch this reality-feeling, they would be believed in in spite of criticism, even though they might be vague and remote to be almost unimaginable..." (ibid:58). We are no longer able to simply accept the experiences of others without the validity text of like experience or empirical veracity. Nor should we, says James. But what needs be done is to include the subjective within the objectives of science, and psychology, given its focus on the individual mind and its agencies, is the most likely place to begin such an extension of the sciences as a whole.

The reams of examples included in James's work confirming that persons experience the abnormative in a number of ways is enough to conclude that at the very least, our imagination is capable of the most extraordinary convolutions and reconstructions of "normal" sense perception. But if it can do so, what is the guarantee that our waking and alert senses are undisturbed in their empirical faculties? Why, in other words, is the routine world considered to be more real than some other reality? For sociology, it is simply because of majority rule. This means not merely that most people most of the time experience the world in readily identifiable ways—it is mainly an external realm filled with objects of both natural and human manufacture, and consists of symbols which human beings can interpret and act upon—and that other versions of reality are not sponsored as fully by our fellow humans. In extreme cases, we encounter "cults" where the worldview is so altered by the in-group that the extremity of ideas often can led to extreme actions. Usually, whatever hallucinatory appeals the potentially viable other world makes upon us can be over the longer term ignored, however shaken, intrigued, or apprehensive we may be about them in the moment of encounter. And we would well question not merely their veracity in some lay scientific manner, but their very rationality as relevant to our lives. James states baldly that they are relevant to us at an ontological level, but he does not go so far to suggest that they are predicative of future experience. That is, the fact that we experience alternate realities within this one is not to be taken as a foreshadowing that there exists other worlds apart from this one. Yet the very presence of not only subjective experiences which do not "fit" easily into the normative patterns of social life, as well as the presence of philosophical texts which attempt to account for such phenomena, point us squarely in the direction of a new conception of the afterlife, the one with which we are discussing presently. It is a distinctly modern belief to assure oneself that consciousness does continue, but without any of the baggage of judgement or evaluation that adhered for our ancestors. Even the major twentieth-century philosopher Hans-Georg Gadamer suggested in an interview late in life that he believed that although he had no religious beliefs and took no comfort in the idea of God, that "this was not all there was to life, and that there was more to consciousness than we yet knew from this life." Others have stated that we live in an age of faith, but not belief.

These kinds of ideas are recent, as we have seen, but they do approximate the way in which most of us do live, at least in the "developed" world. This is so because we have also recently developed the revolutionary idea that the world can be made a better place. There is no need to wait for a journey to the other world, nor is there a need to wait for the other world to make its appearance in our own, as some versions of the apocalypse predict. "Progress" is certainly an idea that itself is regarded with justified suspicion in our own day, although our recent ancestors celebrated it as the inevitable triumph of what they regarded as both superior intellect and technology, as well as the best society vanquishing lower forms of cultural evolution, this patently nineteenth century ideology was what gave rise to the theory of organismic evolution. Interest in the cultural variety of progression—though with a distinct purpose outside of itself that Darwin did not buy into—had preceded the biological version for many decades. We have become judges of our own world, and proceed to judge what is in this life. There is no afterword or afterthought to the world that we know, and if there is, we are not subject to its judgement. Better still, such an afterlife that is both a continuation of consciousness without any kind of extra-human evaluation is the most convenient version of any such belief as it allows us to rest with confidence that we will not so much die as be transformed and continue. The fear of both death and judgement is taken away in this version of the afterlife, and we have been able to construct such a model because of our thoroughgoing belief in the evaluative character of the life we lead while still alive and in human form. Organic society, with its attendant hierarchies and division of labor, demands of us that we judge continuously and also subject ourselves to the judgement of others. No other world would be worth believing in at all if it still included yet more judgement, however more profound such might be imagined to be.

There remain two further observations that underscore the idea of unevaluated continuity. The first may be seen as an extension of

James's thesis that other realities may well be present to consciousness but are accessed in a manner that differs from normal sensory perception. Dementia and other diagnoses kindred with it are certainly poignant and pathetic in the suffering they cause their victims, but James would demand that we observe such symptoms as scientifically and objectively as possible, and use all possible theoretical models to aid in our understanding of them. Although the usual clinical reaction to dementia is that it is a projective pathology having its roots in a diseased brain, there is another current theory regarding its manifestation that comes not from psychology, but from physics. Dementia causes persons to believe they are living in some kind of alternate reality, where persons who are dead are not dead, and persons who live in our world were never even born in those alternate. Hallucinations concerning such phenomenon have a palpability that is very distracting to victims and disconcerting to their loved ones, whose perception remains squarely and continuously in the usual normative world. Hundreds of thousands of cases report this shifting of realities. Is it only that these persons are experiencing wish-fulfillment and delusory hallucinations, or is there something more interesting—and something with more profound implications than simply "losing one's mind"—involved in this phenomenon?

"Superstring" theory may provide an alternative understanding of dementia that, although difficult to investigate by known methods, may at least be existentially provocative, and may help us treat those suffering with the diagnosis with more seriousness and compassion. The fundamental building blocks of matter are said to be made up of strings of sub-atomic particles that vibrate at specific harmonics. One popular version of the theory proposes ten different dimensions to the universe, but it is important to note that there are about ten to the five-hundredth power versions of possible theories that would account for the observable evidence so far available to us through linear accelerators and particle physics experiments. Alternate dimensions unavailable to our usual human sense perception are not only proposed by such theories, but are mathematically predicted by them. There is nothing in any of this that suggests we might be able to sense other dimensions of reality, let alone that these other dimensions, once sensed, would be populated by other versions of the world we have come to know and love as our own. That is, the mathematics of superstring theory do not include the sentiment that different harmonic vibrations of fundamental particles create different worlds that might house alternate time-lines or human destinies. But what is included in such theories is the mathematics for the presence of alternate or "higher" dimensions that are contiguous with our own. That is, they occupy "space-time" along with our usual four dimensions—the three large spatial dimensions plus time or duration—though they are difficult to imagine for us as three-dimensional spatial beings.

If our brains are altered to detect different harmonic resonances than those considered to be usual—an idea first implied by James's theory of alternate but contiguous forms of consciousness—there is no reason to think that such alternate realities might not have an existence perfectly well ordered and fully present as our own. What they might consist of is of course another matter, and it is highly speculative to simply declare that these other possible dimensions would be immediately recognizable to us as simply different timelines in which the lost loved ones of this world might well live on and have different fates. Yet with ten to the five-hundredth power of possible versions of superstring theory untested and by and large analytically unexplored there is room for at least a reasoned imagination to guide us. Most importantly, the compassionate interest in taking seriously someone else's experiences as not merely subjective and decayed, but as intersubjective and intriguing, is a first step on the road to an ethics of care for both the other and for oneself. We too, who do not yet suffer dementia but might well do so in our declining years have desires no different than those who may well be seen as fulfilling them through the visions of a possible extra-dimensionality.

One important pattern to the cases of hallucinatory reports concerning diagnoses of dementia is that there seems to be just as many instances of the loss of loved ones as their recovery. That is, events which we would not wish to be true do appear to have transpired in these other realities—a child was never born, for example, or someone has died who in our world is very much alive, in the same way that others who are dead are resurrected by the visions—and this suggests a certain objectivity to the experiences. If they were purely sentimentally driven, we would expect the alternate dimension to be more like a kind of latter-day mathematical paradise where everything and everyone we wish for is included without exception. That this is manifestly not the case points at least in part to the idea of alternate dimensions that include their own timelines, vibrating at a different harmonic than what we expect from the structure of the cosmos we have grown used to.

The realm of modern scientific analysis in its relation to the idea of unevaluated continuity is not limited to mathematical theory. The second instance of current experience is one of direct observation of something apparently unexpected and odd. By the late 1970s, technology was available to place microscopic cameras inside the body. One experiment placed them in a dying person, and did so in anticipation of the moment of death. The astonishing event that was recorded—and which the author himself saw in a television series about the human body that aired around 1979—was that at the moment of expiration, millions of tiny "bubbles" were let loose from all parts of the body. The narrator commented on this and then said, somewhat mysteriously, "No one yet knows what they are." I recall distinctly staring at the screen with my parents, and uttering simply, "The soul." My parents were as astonished at me, then thirteen or so, as they were at the view on the television, and I also recall their staring at me in rapt silence for a few moments. Despite my naive and immediately religious interpretation, it was clear that what I really meant was some description of the life-force, which I then thought was an idea that had not only ethical merit but was likely to be a fact. All children, who know nothing of either their own deaths or even that of others in terms of the profundity of the event, are given to the suggestion that life simply continues. It is, after all, all they have yet experienced. Not only the experiment, but its findings and my interpretation are all related to the overwhelming sensibility that we desire for there to be an afterlife, and that we should attempt to prove its existence to ourselves before we are forced to encounter its potential horizon. Yet the experiment was based on a simple "let's see what happens" motif which is one of the hallmarks of an open science. What was observed was clearly unexpected, and inexplicable. Akin to life, then, our experience of dying can contain nothing other than the unexpected and the yet-to-be-experienced. The idea of an afterlife that is a simple extension of what we have experienced is testament to the sense that for some, at least, the world is worth living in, that life retains its sacred nature, and that we embody only the part of life that is necessary for us to live in the world as it is. If other worlds exist, other ways of living in them are implied. It is this implication that animates not only our passion for life, but our compassion in the face of death.

6
Everything as Not Anything— Nothingness

We know plenty about what dying is; we can know nothing of death. Is this because there is 'nothing' to know? An affirmative response to this question will occupy us for the rest of this chapter. If we took the concept of nothingness too literally, we would of course find nothing but blank pages below, as if one had been arrested in the very writing of life. Yet the concept of nothingness is not itself nothing. We may not be able to imagine pure negation, but indeed we cannot imagine a pure state of anything, present or non-present. Nothingness is rather a combination of anxiety and the uncanny, and it is to this duet of human apprehensiveness that one can begin to address the problem that the fifth and final version of the afterlife presents to us.

Even here, in our most somber and rationalist mood, we are aware that the physical sciences do not espouse nothing, as such. The reduction and breakdown of the human form into its constituent parts presupposes that there is not a consciousness that transcends, transforms, or transfigures itself. They do not presuppose that matter and energy fade into oblivion. Indeed, the transformation of both is what animates much of modern science and their combinations have given us the most detailed insights regarding the structure of the cosmos we have yet known. The body decays, consciousness is lost, humanity is no more. But the matter of which we are made, the post-modern clay of now-unearthly vessels, continues apace. It is well known, though perhaps trivial and amusing, that we are not even ourselves, choate and singular, while alive. We are constantly losing atoms to the space around us, and billions of like particles invade our "bodies," pass through us, add themselves to our forms, only to drop off moments later. We are in a "state of constant flux," to once again abuse this paradoxical adage. In a room of crowded people, we share intimately with all of them at the smallest of levels, the stuff of our very lives. This atomic disarticulation is seen of course to be only the portent of ultimate disintegration. Upon death, the body, if not already beset by denigrating illness and loss of elemental functions and faculties, begins to decay and break apart.

I once had occasion to study an introductory book on Zen Buddhist meditation. The opening exercise went something like this: Imagine yourself dead and gone. Imagine your body disintegrating and coming apart at the seams, slowly, gradually, so that one, if conscious of it, would barely note its passing on. This is what happens in life. Death and life are the same in this way. Imagine your muscles turning to gelatin, your bones to powder, and everything you once were becoming again one with the earth, and ultimately the stars. Quite a journey, given that we have our origins in the starry void, and that we should return there full circle. Sagan famously reminds us that we are "star-stuff" contemplating the stars. Our contemplation then extends to the resurrection of our particulate mass as forms of energy and light, the very basis of all life.

We saw much earlier that the Buddhist "sky burial" mimics the disintegration of the body while also, through the vultures' ascents, mimicking the return of the energy of which we are to the heavens. Zen thought experiments aside, it is clear that many cultures both near and far to our own have a sense that the cosmos is our home and that we must in time return to the place of our collective birth. The birthright of humanity as a whole is not called into question, therefore, by the seeming nihilism of the afterlife as nothingness. Rather, seen in this light, the idea of nothingness affirms most profoundly the circle of life. We do not continue as ourselves or as any other form of sentient being, but we are immortal through the founding Gemini of matter and energy, a union of unlike forms that has created the apparent rarity of consciousness.

Contemplating nothingness, then, does not necessarily involve a loss per se, though we would well mourn the transformation of what is unutterably complex into what is utterly simple. The idea of continuation as a small, non-sentient cloud of elementary particles, hydrogen and helium, iron and oxygen, may not inspire us all that much. We cannot know this kind of continuation, and its return—for it does return in uncountable ways, even if the manner of its return is indubitably accountable through the methods of physics—is also forever closed to us as now conscious beings. Yet we can still be inspired at the grandness and eloquence of this ultimate passage, which recreates the origin of all things. Unlike Berger's ideas regarding "signals of the transcendent," we need know no sentimental journey to understand the basic processes of the creation. But akin to James's concepts and records of abnormative experiences, anxiety and uncanniness indicate the presence of this journey of something conscious made of what it is not, to the nothing of something that in fact is very much not mere nothingness. Human anxiety regarding the uncanny is a trepidation of the encounter with Nothing. The German philosopher Martin Heidegger famously remarked that what had disturbed his consciousness was not something at all, but that "It was Nothing." As indicated by the capital letter, he was suggesting to us that nothing be made into a proper noun, that it should be in fact the name of something. And indeed this something is the most palpable of all things, breaking into our routine reverie as a thief in the night. Death is merely one guise of it, and that it should be so named only underscores its own strange vitality.

There is a realm in which Nothing appears regularly, sidling up beside us, and taking us aback. The uncanny as a form of human experience of precisely our inexperience occurs most often to us as an aesthetic experience, whether of already-designated art objects, derelict houses, or stranded and decaying boats, gravestones etched with the names of those who are also now nothing, or corpses. The curious feeling of apprehension of that what appears to be dead still yet has life, but a form of life eldritch and even menacing to us—Does the altered misery of abandonment also want company?—turns us from exploring too intimately the inner reaches of these places and things. Of course, human curiosity sometimes overcomes the curious in the world. This primate and primal predilection of our species is one of its great strengths, but it also can lead us down the garden path once in a while. What form does the garden of the uncanny take, and where does it take us? These glades glisten with an ichor that slides both upwards to the shadowy firmament, punctuated by bright pot lights of distant suns, as well as to the earth below, the humus of what has gone before us.

Let us, for the remainder of this chapter, take a walk in such a garden, but let us choose the one where the unspeakable sense of loss is merged and ameliorated with the full presence of wonder and joy, for human life is not fundamentally about loss. While alive, we come to know the rehearsal of death well, through the myriad of farewells both heartfelt and of the "good riddance" variety. It is in art, and the aesthetic feelings of a new world that it arises in us, that we find the closest mirror for life. Art may indeed mimic life, but living itself is akin to an art form, given its complexity and the adaptations we must make in the face of new experience. The living out of memory and anticipation is captured in the work of art as an aesthetic object. It has been given life, and in turn, returns this gift to the onlooker, who encounters it as a mere subject, only to be transfigured into a kind of object, one that is both subjected to the work of art—we must endure its presence, especially if it promotes the strange and unheard-of into our lives—as well as being able to object to it—we can resist its influence, but in doing so we have acknowledged its power.

Art often appears otherworldly. Its vision seems not of this reality, but of something beyond. Its guide is occlusive, even deliberately coy. What it sees it sees for us, but does it let us observe the entirety of its truth? Vision is itself an attempt at revelation outside of the limits of sight, and can come across to us as having its own form of dogmatism that ironically limits our ability to see its virtues. But at the same time the naked sword of vision cuts through the stuff of this world, and stands alone on the horizon it has alone created.

One of the insights the vision of art presents to us is a fuller understanding of the moment of this world's motion. It is well known that certain works freeze or capture such moments—the painting of scenes as tableaux, the sculpture as pose, the musical work as the expression of a single emotion untrammelled by distraction—but beyond these more transparent and referential examples there is also the moment of the world's being which is more rarely related to our being in the world as it is. Indeed, this kind of vision often suggests to us that there is either more to life than we usually give it credit for, or that there is extant, contiguous but not overlapping with it, another life, qualitatively different, and to which access is restricted. The role of art in the lives of worldly persons takes on a function similar to species of religion. That the this-world is richer than its mundane life suggests is kindred with the world extending salvation doctrines of Western belief systems such as Islam and Christianity. The next world is linked to this one as its ideal extension, and one must perform the arts of humanity on earth to move beyond their sullied place and fallen state. That the this-world may be overcome in its entirety is kindred with the world denying transcendentalities of the Eastern systems, such as Buddhism. The next world may be attained only by vanquishing the this-world from one's spirit and vision. Either way, we are involved in an attempt to better ourselves, to make ourselves more beautiful.

Nazism was hardly the first incarnation that the world may be made a better place through the violence of expurgative death, although it was the first to link this idea specifically with art and thus make it into both an aesthetics and an ideology. The risk that may then immediately be understood when one experiences art as something possessing the uncanniness of the encounter with the "Nothing" is that it proffers to special persons the seer of its vision. In other words, akin to religious revelation, the ones who undergo the transformative rite of passage of visionary art might well think that they have been specifically chosen for such an increase in being because they already have some extensive and expansive version of humanity bred into them. If this breeding is associated with anything other than art itself, the consequences of this belief will be disastrous for all humanity. This is the truest lesson of the uncanny in art.

With art, however, we do not need to decide whether or not it is the case that the mundane world needs be overcome or merely extended. Art gives us the option of continuing to live in the world, our being itself both overcome and extended, as in the hermeneutic experience. The transformational quality of the aesthetic encounter is enough to push us on to a new version of ourselves, as well as having the ability to preserve what it is already about us that will serve as the ground for the growth of the new. The seeds, the earth, the water, and the sun are contained within the aesthetic experience. What the character of this new species of life will be is of course shaped by many other things, but nowhere else, it seems, do we find the confluence of the ingredients of new life more intensely focused than in the presentiment of art.

Yet to encounter art in this way means something different than that of either a concrete future-oriented project or a memorialization. With these, art has offered itself to us in a still instrumental form, or at least, a form that we can turn to the use of the extension of ourselves in the world of forms and objects in which art is merely one category of experience. That is, with self-projection, we extend our would-be beings into the world writ larger than we had been written before, and with self-preservation, we extend our beings back into the history of how they have been, represencing ourselves and making the world larger in its temporal scope. In encountering the uncanniness of art, however, we are extended into a completely new aspect of the world that was hitherto unknown to us, or unknowable by us. We have no ulteriority here, and indeed, this kind of experience with art makes us feel rather that there is an ulterior nature to art itself, one more mysterious and at the same time more truthful and ultimately more real than the usual run of social realities that we inhabit. This new way of being towards the real usually has a profound remonstrative effect on us, either in the sense of the quasi-moral—one needs to live better or be better than one has, given the new vision of art's overcoming of pettiness—or the existential—"I am much more than I gave myself credit for, but this error of estimation is not my fault." The uncanniness of art's presence in the world reminds us, perhaps more than anything else, of its usual absence in our lives. We may feel remorse or regret at this news, for knowledge about the absence of the "larger truth" is itself not usually taken as good news. But this simple relation of presence and absence does not fully describe the effect of art's uncanniness. Indeed, the oddly circumspect but also invasive and trembling presence of that very absence—we now know it to be true that we have been absented by the presence of Being, that upon our stage has trod only beings like ourselves, and those too much like ourselves have been our interlocutors—is rather better described as "non-presence." There is something missing from both our vision and from our consciousness. Yet we are not immediately comprehending of just exactly what this absence signifies regarding its substance.

"What is the matter?" is a common enough query asked by our compatriots when they have observed in us the charge of the uncanny, but it is just this kind of question that lacks the definitive and substantial response of referentiality. We are, in fact, not at all sure what all this was about, or what has just transpired. We do know, however, that we have been altered, that our substance was originally lacking and it was this absence of the stuff of truth or of beauty, the good or the spirit, et cetera, that put us "at risk" for the encounter with an overabundance, sometimes playful and sometimes playing. This knowledge itself has its own trembling uncanniness about it, or better, it is our understanding of ourselves as part of the general absence of our ideals in both our lives and in the world that stuns us with the resonance of the uncanny, as it often takes some time after such experiences to "shake them off," as it were.

The analysis of art through a phenomenology of the uncanny must proceed from this fact alone: that the experience of non-presence uncovers the absence of presence in being and world. There are categories of what was "supposed" to be present, and what was supposedly present within these aesthetic encounters, as we will see below. But whatever we may make of what we are missing—have we been morally culpable, are we living in ugliness or self-deprecation, do we know only other versions of ourselves as other persons, are we simply "uncultured" and ignorant?—it is the radicality of the new "knowingness" that the presentiment of art makes fully present to us that we must confront. Simply put, we are confronted by art as the beings we have been, without recourse to the use of art as a way in which our beings might concretely improve themselves, either through rewriting themselves as part of the larger world or by giving ourselves a dedicated auto-history. It is this feeling of insubstantiality, borne on the currents that whisk us away from all solid projects or monuments, that disconcerts us the most. We have been shown up to be less than we had thought in a powerful way, but we are not at all sure how to proceed with remedying the situation, and we often end by questioning the value or the relevance of the uncanny, just as culturally we have at length begun to question the once-presumed existence of the otherworldly itself.

But what is the nature and effect of aesthetic uncanniness? We can speak of it in a number of ways: "The poetic image is a sudden salience on the surface of the psyche…" says the French philosopher of aesthetics, Gaston Bachelard (Bachelard 1964:xi [1958]). It is the "opposite of causality," for "in this reverberation, the poetic image will have a sonority of being. The poet speaks on the threshold of being" (ibid:xiii). Anything that interrupts the general run of living on can appear as uncanny, which, after all, has its base meaning in the experience of the abnormative. No other meaning need originally be ascribed to what is deviant, other than a transgression that is part of the norm and not at all alien to it. At the same time, we are seldom content to leave it there. The cliquish and obfuscatory attempts of Romantic period occultists who tell us that "there are things you should not know" remind us of nothing more than the early Pythagoreans, protecting the sacred mysteries of the square root of two or other "irrational" numbers. This kind of defense of the would-be uncanny has no merit. No, the uncanniness of human experience, though rare when compared with the wide-awake-everydayness of the quotidian, nevertheless has something profound to speak to us about concerning what it means to be fully human, and art attests to this dimension of being which, for a moment, coincides with the Being of beings in the world.

If Freud noted that within art there was something alive and sonorous beyond the formal content as well as the form of media of the work, and at the same time having its source of action not in our own normative observation of the work of art—one says to oneself, "I am in a gallery to see art," etc.—then we might also describe this dimension of being as being able to be at the threshold of itself. That same liminal space which we have heard the poet speak of is the step into the house of aesthetic experience. The American philosopher, Gregg Horowitz, notes, "This is the uncanniness of art that needs interpretation by a psychical work that is never done. It is, we might say, the traumatic kernel of historical knowledge" (cf. Horowitz 2001:119ff). It is troublesome because it constitutes precisely an interruption of the flow of living on, but not one critical enough to be fatal to the threat of being itself. Though it is a "...minor crisis, this crisis on the simple level of a new image, contains the entire paradox of a phenomenology of the imagination, which is: how can an image, at times very unusual, appear to be a concentration of the entire psyche?" (Bachelard 1964:xiv [1958]). What power does it have to break through the normative run, and "...react on other minds and in other hearts, despite all the barriers of common sense, all the disciplined schools of thought, content in their immobility?" (ibid:xv). The answer appears to lie within the question. It is the very immobility, not of thinking nor of thought itself, but of discourse and paradigm, either socialized as the culture or learned as a higher culture, that blockades the entrance to any liminal space.

We are too human in our discourses, in the sense that the fully socialized human being is a co-conspirator employed at the local social prison. If we are to become as well humane, then we must pay heed to what unsettles the order of social reality and presents a reality that human science must also interpret, but that the rest of us can ignore if we wish: "This pre-human way of seeing things is the painter's way. More completely than lights, shadows, and reflections, the mirror image anticipates within things, the labor of vision," suggests the French phenomenological philosopher, Maurice Merleau-Ponty (Merleau-Ponty 1964:168 [1961]). It is this interiority of art that lends itself to our perception that the uncanny is something hidden, only partially exposed in the aesthetic encounter, alluded to, but included within our conscious horizon as one glimpses the loom of a distant ship through the binoculars when looking out to sea. But it is not art that occludes. The hiddenness of our beings is hidden within us, and is brought into the lighted space of being through the aesthesia of encounters with works of art. This "state of grace," opposed to the semi-conscious anesthesia of living on, confers upon us not a privilege of salvation—as was assumed in the pre-modern spaces of the sacred associated with religion and all of the works of art that had as their purpose the increase of only the Being of their gods—but the grace through which we can endure the struggles of daily life.

It is this experience of art, apparently eldritch and even threatening, as an event in a Lovecraftian romance, which actually brings into focus not only the force of art as a lens for life, but for all of the rest of our lives no matter how artless and petty, in a meaningful manner. Art reminds us that life too has meaning. Art is the source, not for life's meaning, but for the uncanny nature of life to be given meaning when life itself is too preoccupied with arranging meaningfulness into norms. The German social philosopher, Alfred Schutz, states, "There is one fact that shows that most of my actions do have meaning. This is the fact that, when I isolate them from the flux of experience and consider them attentively, I then do find them to be meaningful in the sense that I am able to find in them an underlying meaning" (Schutz 1967:19 [1932]). No experience is entirely without meaning, Schutz concludes, given that in order to reflect upon an event, we must participate in the key phase of "having an experience" to make it meaningful for ourselves, rather than merely experiencing events with no further thought about them. And yet the irruptive quality of the uncanny, whether experienced through art or some other abnormative social context, while at once still social upon reflection, is not immanently so. The "intuition of essences," is not all at once appropriated by the social scene, in the same way that the neighbor cannot immediately become the socius in order for her to render an authenticity to a radical other to herself. So the uncanny must still be explicated along the lines of a study of the phenomenon as they are, and not only a social phenomenology that looks at how human beings interact with objects and other people. What lies between these two forms of thought is aesthetics in its phenomenological and phenomenonical understandings.

We can proceed from events that are apparently immediate and transparent. Gadamer suggests that "what a gesture expresses is 'there' in the gesture itself. A gesture is something wholly corporeal and wholly spiritual at the same time. The gesture reveals no inner meaning behind itself. The whole being of the gesture lies in what it says" (Gadamer 1986:79 [1977]). We can proceed here as social beings as if we know the whole story. This is, in base and relatively anonymous form, how social relations operate. We stereotype the other as a category. We do not need to know them as a person. We do the same for social interaction, hardly heeding the depths of wellspring for each and every person's behaviors, though a detailed genealogy would reveal a more authentic pattern to social life. The pragmatics of living on dictate these courses to us, and, akin to the discourses, we are content to leave well enough alone. It is enough of a challenge, admittedly, for each one of us to face the uncanny ability of life to waylay the "best laid of plans." So a phenomenology of the aesthetics of being in the world need not be a harbinger of a homiletic. This new knowledge of self-understanding that we seek through art can be taken as a fresh perspective. It may indeed change our lives so that our reflections match our experiences—so that thoughts catch up with truths—but it alone cannot make the difficult decisions for us. This other level, where reflection must always and already become self-reflection, imposes itself upon us when we consider that there is in fact nothing so transparent about even mundane social reality: "At the same time every gesture is also opaque in an enigmatic fashion. It is a mystery that holds back as much as it reveals. For what the gesture reveals is the being of meaning rather than the knowledge of meaning" (ibid.).

It is, in fact, the depth of social interaction in everyday reality that sets the stage for the profundity of art, for we are very often introduced for the first time to the subtlety of the former only through the latter. Unlike science, however, our subjective encounter with the work of art does not provide as sure a guarantor of predictive certainty. Its presence must rest within our own, and we may well include it as part of the decision-making that must occur in ethical spheres of social action. Just because the nature of the work of culture is given a kind of pre-givenness through art should not suggest that this clarity is fully portable across social spheres, say, from that aesthetic to that ethical. If it is true that in the realm of artistic expression "...there is no need for a code or convention of interpretation; the meaning is as inherent in immediate experience as is that of a flower garden," as we are reminded by the famous American philosopher of education and pragmatist, John Dewey (Dewey 1980:83 [1934]), then it is equally true that the flowers in that garden have been socially arranged—the very term "garden" refers to such a construct—and that implies directly that there must be a prior and rather formal code by which we can understand the experience to be an immediate one, and not one of or requiring further reflection. This is all too similar to the surface debate between empiricism and rationalism, where experience, the source of all knowledge, is questioned along the lines of the nature of human experience: "What must there be in order to have an experience (at all)?" we might ask: "Whatever is alive has its source of movement within itself and has the form of self-movement. Now play appears as a self-movement that does not pursue any particular end or purpose so much as movement as movement, exhibiting so to speak a phenomenon of excess, of living self-representation. And in fact that is just what we perceive in nature..." (Gadamer 1986:23 [1977] italics the text's). Even such a phenomenon has its uncanniness rooted in the fact that we expect some source of movement that could be demonstrated to be external to the object or to the organism.

How is it that we even have a consciousness, let alone a reflective and duplicative one? How is it that the movement of beings corresponds to that of the nature of Being? Without the metaphysics of an idealism which suggests form regulates and "predates" both appearance and content, an understanding that cannot in itself explain the concept of form or the cosmogony of the prime mover other than that of a regressive creation, one must look for the apparently unlikely and strangely present non-presence of being within one's own perception: "...this sense is immanent in the sensuous being its very organization. The sensuous is given first and sense is regulated by it," says the French phenomenological philosopher, Mikel Dufrenne (Dufrenne 1973:12 [1953]). Immanence is a characteristic of the sacred as well as of the irruptive. In such a sense as that phenomenological, immanence is the character of what cannot be characterized merely as sense, or through the sensate structure of consciousness. Ritual, vision, the solidarity of prayer, the many-tongued voices of diverse tensions, come to find a home in the succor of the hypostasized community, what is imagined to be the better version of that which we possess on earth. All these we search for in art. But they confront us most precisely with the sudden presence of the uncanny that is already within the relationship between art and its public. Art confronts the individuated observer and forces him to consider becoming a double; both as the other in the work, but also as another observer who also encounters the same work.

Art serves the aggrandized purpose of ritual for a society that is suspicious of the politics and normative social control of ritual: "A work of art elicits and accentuates this quality of being a whole and of belonging to the larger, all-inclusive, whole which is the universe in which we live. This fact, I think, is the explanation of that feeling of exquisite intelligibility and clarity we have in the presence of an object that is experienced with esthetic intensity. It explains also the religious feeling that accompanies intense esthetic perception" (Dewey 1980:195 [1934]). Yet just because we have the feeling of intensity does not mean we have any formal clarity as to what exactly is possessing us. Indeed, it is this "oceanic feeling" that Freud famously disdains that contains all of the vastness of the cosmos, yet also all of the vagueness that is echoed in reflection with others about the event after it has been experienced. Persons communicate "as if" what they knew was the same thing, or as if their experiences of it generated the same feelings and meaning for them. All of this, in sober second light or apart from the group, or without the markers of art itself, seems quite unlikely, even romantic. So we are left with the sense that what has occurred has indeed done so at the expense of full and certain knowledge of it, and could have only occurred in this manner, whatever rationalizations may be supplied later on. We must come to the conclusion that "something in art must resist coming to conceptual clarity despite sustained reflection on it, and so art must be the bearer, not just of instance of the uncanny, but of the dynamic of uncanniness itself" (Horowitz 2001:126–7). Certainly in modernity, art often ironically appears as the most normative experiential space in which to go searching for the abnormative. Indeed, this serious journey can be co-opted by fetish and market, as well as rationalized settings of observation as in the Louvre or the Vatican, where guided tours take the place of self-reflection. Because these spaces where art is archived, the modern reliquaries of the sacred objects, are socially sanctioned spaces of deviance and subjectivity, it is possible that they ultimately defeat the very thrust of the uncanny with the parry of the hyper-rational.

Yet the sensibility of such places should not impinge on the things that they house and sanctify. Their utter spatiality is itself a sign that one needs some room to negotiate new chambers of the heart of beings. Present fullness demands of us that we also fully attend to the present in which we encounter the gift of consciousness writ large. The task falls to us more fully when we attempt to link the uncanny with the context in which it apparently occurred: "It is impossible to understand perception as the imputation of a certain significance to certain sensible signs, since the most immediate sensible texture of these signs cannot be described without referring to the object they signify" (Merleau-Ponty 1964:51 [1948]).

Our very objection to the uncanny—in the form of alienated being, of homesickness, or discomfort that exclaims within us that we wish to return to what we know, or can know—is the first and necessary part of action directed toward the object or the work of art that brings it into our field of sensibility. We know first and foremost that it is strange to us, but even this zero degree of experience allows all further ones to evolve. What the ends are include a new knowledge that part of our very selves was also strange to us, and that part of ourselves may well be strange to others. In this estrangement of the uncanny we are made unfamiliar to what we have been. This is essentially the characteristic of all hermeneutic experience, such as that it at first overcomes prior prejudice by ignoring it, by pretending that it did not exist. In this way, the uncanny short-circuits our expectations, both of our own reactions and of what art might or should be like. It forces us to scramble in front of it, its play is unforeseen, and we have no immediate defense against it. As with the once unfamiliar images of modernist painting, "we must make an active contribution of our own and make an effort to synthesize the outlines of the various planes as they appear on the canvas. Only then, perhaps, can we be seized and uplifted by the profound harmony and rightness of a work, in the same way as readily happened in earlier times on the basis of pictorial content common to all" (Gadamer 1986:8 [1977]). If in agrarian societies there was an aesthetic solidarity more mechanical than in our own, it was still the narrative that images portrayed—as if the momentary morality of this or that symbolic juxtaposition, the Knight and Death, or St. Jerome and the Lion, etc.—was at once part of a larger ongoing narrative but also, and more importantly, could leap out of such a syntagmatic chain of signifiers and become the most salient of significant symbols. The uncanniness of pre-modern art assumes one knows the story well, and thus is prepared in a very different sense for a sudden vision or revelatory inspiration that might occur in its presence. Yet further back, the great pilgrimages of the medieval period attested to the profound desire on the part of human beings to indeed encounter aesthesis in the form of itself as a sacred subspecific. Art in the service of an organized belief system was able, through the experience of its awesome vaults and spires, to transcend the mere norms of ritual and worship which also took place in the same spaces and within the gaze of the same works of art. Rituals of all kinds being as well theater, need their stages, props, scripts, and actors. But it is the setting that backdrops and allows the scene to transport us outside of the mundane spheres of social life that have their contrasting settings. At the same time, the sacred is only understandable as something from within which the uncanny may present itself if we do not completely forget the social scenery where such events occur much more rarely: "The builder, then, does not set apart and enclose a void, but instead a certain dwelling place of forms, and, in working on space, he models it, within and without, like a sculptor," says the French art historian, Henri Focillon (Focillon 1989:76 [1934]). Insofar as architecture is akin to the organ of musical instruments in its relations to other art media, the architect is the composer of spaces, spaces through which time is diverted in its regular flow in calculated ways. There is a damming up of the tensions between past and present, and thus a more intense character of life can be presented there. We are more aware of our connections with the tradition and with the dead, that is, two things or ideas that are considered to have passed, or to be the past, rather than as part of the something of the present, in these places than in any others. "He is a geometrician in the drafting of a plan, a mechanic in the assembling of a structure, a painter in the distribution of visual effects and a sculptor in the treatment of masses" (ibid.). When we, at long last, weary of the regularity of the flow of temporal life and its necessary routines, enter both into and unto such a space, we are ourselves opened up by its architecture. We become more intimate with its surroundings in the same way that we become greater adepts and acolytes regarding self-understanding. Other humans created this place, but once created its voice is that of both their collective labors but as well, holds within its chorus a new voice, far older, of the tradition and what may lie beyond it. We are emptied of our quotidian cares, we are shaken from our ennui, we are uplifted from our marginality, and we are arrested in our imagination. We are presented with the words of life writ large, with a textuality as ancient as the social contract, though in a grandiose and static form: "The reader of the Text may be compared to someone at loose end (someone slackened off from any imaginary); this passable empty subject strolls—it is what happened to the author of these lines, then it was that he had a vivid idea of the Text—on the side of a valley...," says the French literary critic, Roland Barthes (Barthes 1977:159 [1971]).

Here, then, is a recipe for the abiding taste of the other-world. But the notion of the threshold for which art is the handmaiden does not include all forms of the uncanny. And in fact the uncanny relies heavily on our imaginations, cultural as these are, but also personal and based on specific sets of experiences no one else has quite been involved with as have we. If part of that which we are to understand as part of ourselves is that we, too, within the interiority of being in the world, possess and are possessed by the uncanny, then this other part of our being takes the form of a character from the other-world. Even in modernity, it is the unconscious that speaks to us of this relation metaphorically, but as well the patterned symbolic structure of the culture of the day; the train, for instance, no longer augurs a guise of death to us as trains have faded from the actual landscape, have become quaint rather than threatening, and thus have become mute as symbols of the imagination. We thus need a world where its denizens and their scenes have a particular use: "He could use them to elucidate his problems of the union of soul and body. I myself consider literary documents as realities of the imagination, pure products of the imagination. And why should the actions of the imagination not be as real as those of perception?" (Bachelard 1964:158 [1958]). Yet there is a difference here, one that presents itself to us as a different reality.

The order of reality corresponds to the nature of order in worlds that are usually set apart, but yet come together through the human imagination. These worlds might be characterized in a number of ways, nature and culture, the mundane and the extramundane, heaven and earth, etc., but in each dyad the other is always present. Their reality is indeed of an equal stature, but only because they co-mingle. Culture is one of the adaptive results of nature, the judgement of what is extraordinary based on our knowledge of the routine, paradise our ultimate aspiration for this world and not some other. The true difference between the worlds is marked by the manner in which they are presented to our consciousness: "There is no obscurity of feeling, which knows the expressed object, but only for the understanding, which knows the represented object" (Dufrenne 1973, 411 [1953]). As with all things elliptically apophantic, all events that might come to us as epiphanies, it is only our perspective of worlds in collision that allows the feeling of union with the sacred through the vehicle of art's uncanniness to be known without ambiguity.

What we are experiencing truly is different in the sense that it comes to us, not in no uncertain terms, but with no terms other than a negation of the quality of living ever onward towards death. Yet it is our very knowledge of what this latter quality is, both in its overwhelming but finite quantity and its moment by moment ambiguity, that allows the feeling of the uncanny to be ironically transparent: "Such fullness of emotion and spontaneity of utterance come, however, only to those who have steeped themselves in experiences of objective situations; to those whose imaginations have long been occupied with reconstructing what they see and hear. Otherwise, the state is more like one of frenzy in which the sense of orderly production is subjective and hallucinatory" (Dewey 1980:72 [1934]). The full presence of the present is held within the confluence of the attention it takes to focus on the work of art. Since art challenges our mundane expectations, our predictive and predicative assumptions, we are stilled by its presence. We must contemplate its surfaces or its sonorities, and we must then begin to feel our own presence in a world that has itself been stilled. Perhaps what is generally characteristic of the uncanny in art is this lack of motion, almost as if our heart has been stopped and we are close to a kind of death. The temporary absence of the motion of the world and the dynamic that includes ourselves in its motion is oddly disconcerting. There is an aloneness to our experience while at the same time a very clear awareness that we are not alone but have been joined by another voice, perhaps long dormant, which awakens itself through our presence. None of this appears to have anything to do with how we usually live and speak: "There are no commonplace expressions, like gestures or grimaces, of a sense of mass and power, of a delight in nature...and that further explains why expressions of the latter sort are less frequently discussed; they are simply not encountered very often by most people," says the American philosopher of language, Guy Sircello (Sircello 1972:63). If not, perhaps, we would not in fact become so suddenly aware that there has been a shift in the worlding of the world, a movement towards the moment that encapsulates our existence. We are forever held within the now, and just because this will also ever pass on does not negate its only present function of letting us be. There is an immediate analogy to the work of art as it is used subjectively with the kinds of discourse that attempt to hold on to the moment and force its acquiescence to either projection, memory, or identity. But it is the presence of the uncanny that unsettles these ideas of stasis, because it is the uncanny that can arrest the entirety of the world and our being at once, and does not rest upon the contrivance of projects that must remain in a world that passes like clouds.

When art is expressed as what appears to be our everyday language, the effect is even more startling as we are made aware that language itself, even without poetry, entails the essence of being as existence and not stasis: "The intellectualist philosopher who wants to hold words to their precise meaning, and uses them as the countless little tools of clear thinking is bound to be surprised by the poet's daring" (Bachelard 1964:146 [1958]). As with art in general, the truest sign of the uncanny is that it brings us home to reality. What is now made real for us is the fact of our existence and the fact of the world, ever ambiguous and ever passing, and the discomfort we feel in the face of reality is that we can never truly find a home in such a world, never truly become at home in language, unless of course we adopt the uncanny into ourselves. This adoption implies that there is a home for what is homeless in humanity, and that this home is within our own beings. If, as Bachelard continues, "language itself dreams" (ibid.), then the dreamless dream of living on takes place in and as language, and its significance is held within the reality it can construct, always a moving target, already an anonymity and a question.

And this realization takes place not through the language of ordinary speech and writing alone, but in any media in which art finds its own home: "There remains an ineliminable connection between what we like to call the wordless language of music and the verbal language of normal linguistic communication. Perhaps there is also a similar connection between the objective vision with which we orient ourselves in the world, and the claim that art makes upon us both to construct new compositions directly from the elements of the objective visible world and to participate in the profound tensions that they set up" (Gadamer 1986:38–9 [1977]). Very often it takes something other than "normal communication" to get the point across in its fullness of presence. We are, indeed, more often led to rationalize this or that event through the excessive pseudo-interpretation that has its origin in the too often cited idioms of "live and learn" or "that's life."

But just exactly what is this life that we are learning from, and what is it that we learn? Or is it not that we learn to live, rather than the more blithe manner of happenstance such idioms suggest? No doubt we also do not learn, depending on the context, or that we may equally learn not to learn. The fullness of the present's presence presents itself to us as irruptive and unwilling to let us unlearn its lesson. Like anxiety proper, the uncanny, very often seen as a vehicle for the former, has a positive existential function for us. It does not know how to "leave us alone" in the same way as we can demand of other persons or through denial of many of our memories—pride can conquer conscience in this regard, as Nietzsche famously noted—or even social institutions once they are satisfied in their bureaucratic requirements. The uncanniness of the uncanny is that it is ever-present, waiting pensively in the shadows of the everyday, whose light cannot fully illuminate every space of being as it flickers its way to and from its mundane zenith.

What was already present comes only to its full presence in the void of rationalized meanings. Sometimes this presence, and our presence within it, is an abyss, bringing to the fullest consciousness—, which also includes the unconscious and the consciousness of others insofar as they are relevant—our character and role in this or that life event. What occurred is what is now occurring to us. We have felt its whole for the first time. Indeed, the uncanny reminds us that we seldom feel the whole of any part of our lives, as the onrush of time keeps our focus from discerning the true shape of things as they hurtle by, rather like looking at a rushing river. The foreshortening and distanciation of running and coursing water precludes focus, and to rest one's eyes on one spot in the river is to see merely the flow of different waters, constant and continuous. When the aesthetic encounter recreates the work of art as a quasi-subject in the world of both subjects and objects, it immobilizes us as a quasi-object. The effect is often dramatic and transformational, as well as intensely disturbing or yet comfortable, depending on the association: "There is interest in completing an experience. The experience may be one that is harmful to the world and its consummation undesirable. But it has aesthetic quality" (Dewey 1980:39 [1934]). That we need to know only ourselves in such a moment, but that we come to such a self-understanding through the work of others, and, furthermore, that it leads to an understanding of an other which had been effaced or forgotten, are the hallmarks of authentic and dramatic living: "This is the metaphysical reason for the concentration of drama in time, of the condition of unity of time. It is born of the desire to come as close as possible to the timelessness of this moment which is yet the whole of life," says the Hungarian literary critic, Georg Lukacs (Lukacs 1974:158 [1910]).

However full the encounter with art makes the present, it does so by the suggestion that what is present is so by virtue of the movement of being from another kind of time, and from another world than our own. Just as we are judged by the present situations we have created or find ourselves in, we also, by implication, suggest to ourselves that another kind of judgement is also pressing in upon us, and this too emanates from another kind of world or being. The uncanny in art thus confronts us with a set of simple questions: What kind of being? What kind of judgement? What are we to do in the face of the beyond? If the work of art is confronting us with our deficits, it also reaffirms our strengths, and in fact uses both weakness and credit to render its communication to us with greater clarity. Whatever it is we are missing, in other words, art can supply if we are open to its insight. Whatever it is we possess, art can magnify if we are open to transforming our experience and sharing it within the new realm of aesthetic quasi-subjectivity. We need not be, then, too apt in our approximation of this world's flaws when we encounter what we take to be a better world through the windows of the arts. It is not as if we alone embody all the frailties of the human subject in the world. No doubt we each of us have our fair share of them, but art does not personalize in the sense of finding fault with us. One of the major ways in which art touches our being and changes its vision over the generations is that it can have similar effects on many different kinds of persons.

We must surmise, rather, that the aesthetic object now re-presenced in the world as a quasi-subject also takes action in that world, action which transforms its own presence by altering the course of our perceptions. The quasi-subject has a kind of moral volition, and if in its self-representation it takes on the trappings of an intentional stance borrowed from the mythological narratives of the age in which art began its moral career, it does so only to impress upon us its historical as well as its ultimate relevance. We do the same. We are also not embodiments of a morality per se, but remain nevertheless moral beings in a world that has been shaped by the principles of morality and of late, anti-morality. The light or the darkness that we find ensconced as tropes of the other-world are made fully present in this one through the aesthetic encounter. Art makes plain the ideals of good and evil in a world where such a moral spectrum is moribund and sometimes bankrupt. At the same time, art reminds us that even if such a worldview and its evaluations are mute, persons practice a pragmatic version of these judgements regularly, and those who are subject to them feel their consequences to be very real.

This social fact underscores the relevance of an art form that does not abstract itself from the reality of the world, even that reality which is always and already immensely social: "The essence of the beautiful does not lie in some realm opposed to reality. On the contrary, we learn that however unexpected our encounter with beauty may be, it gives us an assurance that the truth does not lie far off and inaccessible to us, but can be encountered in the disorder of reality with all its imperfections, evils, errors, extremes, and fateful confusions" (Gadamer 1986:15 [1977]). Cosmos from chaos, good from evil, art from life, none of these are cosmogonical in character, but rather their relation is contiguous and imbricated. One does not arise from the other, nor is one the source of its metaphysical compatriot. We indeed preserve what we think are the "oughts" of life against "what is," but this does not mean that we only allow such principles to be thought of as by definition foreign to our everyday lives. Even so, we do appear to need a catalyst to bring them together, to experience their similitude that is already present in our beings: "The ontological function of the beautiful is to bridge the chasm between the ideal and the real" (ibid.). If what we think should be the truth is often opposed to what we see the truth to be, then the aesthetic realm is a world in which we have difficulty adjudicating which is which.

This ambiguity is the harbinger of the Nothingness that we imagine we fear. Art seems to be in the same category as other objects that appear to have a life of their own, or at least resonate with the humanity that has come into their creation. We suggested earlier that the oddly living presence of what we call art is akin to the curiously "unliving" presence of human-made objects that have been abandoned, either through long use or mishap. Derelict houses and shipwrecks come to mind here, but even the junked car in a farmer's field can call forth a memory which is not our own. These objects have lived an almost human life, and their presence is testament to this service. Yet they are present in a way that seems to represence life that is already dead, or at least is supposed to be. They haunt our still living landscape, and are a reminder that all things must pass. It is this reminder, this memory of life itself that does not need our biography to situate it, which is the source of their uncanny power. They are the not-quite-mute witness to the fifth and final form of the afterlife, the nothingness that is still something, but a something unlike the things we know and love. We would like to love them and sometimes, with great effort, learn to do so again—hence the rebuilt derelicts on television home renovation shows, the refloated vessels, and the rehabilitated antique vehicles that then, ironically, strive to become "museum quality"—but all of these living efforts stem from the desire to reanimate that which has passed at least once, and sometimes many times.

When I lived in the Mississippi Delta, I occasionally visited the famous antebellum house that had been used as the main prop in the 1950s Hollywood film version of the Tennessee Williams play, *Baby Doll*. It was affectionately known by the locals under that name, the "*Baby Doll* House." While shying away from Williams's often decisive critiques of the Deep South, the house itself was celebrated by local people through the occasional attempt at renovation. Yet by the twenty-first century it had once again fallen into a state of sorry disrepair. The ceiling of the high porch was still painted the traditional sky blue, as if one could look to the heavens from the very house of one's birth. This is the birthright of all human beings, to cross the threshold that makes fragile the separation between life and death. To do so in the course of the everyday marks us as already aware that we must cross and that all of our afterlives are presaged by the fullest absence of what we think we know in life.

7

On Living on after Living

Preparing for an Afterlife

The sea was red and the sky was grey.
I wondered how tomorrow could ever follow today.

—Robert Plant, 1972

Now that we have discussed the afterlife in its five historical forms, what do we then do? Do we simply choose the one that suits us the best and then believe with all our mortal might in it? Are there signs in this life of what is to come? Perhaps these signs, if they exist, might well be yet misread by us? Does everything that we know and love perish without consolation? Do we learn to mourn only so that we can ourselves be mourned?

There are two major ways in which what is dead continues to live on in human history. One concerns the contemporary analyses of artifactual material culture—things of human manufacture that remain long after their creators have died—and are originally of interest only to archaeologists. Like art, artifacts are not seen as mere objects but as vehicles and vessels of the human story in all its wonder and strangeness. The second has to do with the sociological analysis that depersonalized the act of suicide. That is, killing oneself, often seen as a deeply personal, private, and sometimes incomprehensible act, was recast as something that very specific categories of people do with greater frequency than do others of us. Contrary to psychological understandings, which attempt to read the mind of the victim, sociology looked at the wider pattern of exactly what kinds of persons killed themselves. In doing so, suicide became a social, rather than a mere biographical, fact. I want to look in some detail at both of these analyses, beginning with the archaeological one, because they teach us how to prepare for an afterlife no matter its character.

Wylie and Pinsky (1989) attempt to identify some tensions amongst versions of archaeology, joining up the realms of philosophy of science, history, and socio-political critique to the ranks of endeavors undertaken by archaeologists. Within these more recent ideas there remain, however, questions about the efficacy of the disciplinary divisions presented and challenged throughout the texts. Although the atmosphere is different from almost any other book ostensibly dealing with "archaeological" issues, what could have been a much more thought-provoking opportunity for an author's forum is suddenly suspended. There is a specific reason why this is so, a reason that impinges on our current and conflicting beliefs regarding the afterlife.

The editors' introduction tells us that their work and the work of their contributors has a basic epistemological axe to grind, that being a multi-faceted critique of archaeology as only a form of history. A constant thread throughout the texts is the irony extant between archaeology's hopes to establish a singular paradigm under which to work and the later realization that being critical of that which came before them led to an uncritical acceptance of a kind of naive scientism that had already been shown to be problematic even in the physical and life sciences. The editors stress the import of being able to formulate an open-ended series of questions apart from the framework used by many students over the course of much of the course of archaeology. The fact that a single paradigmatic method of practicing archaeology and interpreting archaeological material could not hold together across the discipline made it at once easier and perhaps even more necessary to present such a critique.

For the Canadian philosopher of science, Alison Wylie, the "prehistory" to modern "philosophical analysis" that for many had been an impingement on archaeological territory is included in her summary Arguments against the seemingly solidifying basis of observational empiricism had in fact been around much earlier. Critiques that stress the author function as arbiter towards truth in the manner of an "historical idealism" as well as critiques against and for those studies that contain commitments to theory or ideology are the major themes of her argument. Archaeologists reacted by labelling "philosophy" as a meddler, or its practice detrimental in a general sense, whereas

Wylie wishes to clarify the division between the multitudinous branches of philosophy which until recently had absolutely no interest in archaeological practice, and a very narrow set of interpretations from the philosophy of science which was borrowed by leading archaeologists. Wylie is the only contributor to even hint that such a division is also extant contemporaneously. Although the editors cannot be faulted for other's misunderstandings of the sweep of philosophy, the dual and conflicting effect of manipulating "philosophy" as a critical addition to an archaeology and the misleading scope of philosophical thought and its relation to archaeology is an ironic subtheme underlying many of these kinds of discussions. Particular examples will be highlighted in the following, but suffice it to say for now that "philosophy" is often defined as a "discipline" apart from that of any other. "Philosophy" is seen as having its pragmatic edge defined by the philosophy of science, and presumably other movements and contexts deemed philosophical would be funneled through this department in order to reach "science" as a body apart from what was "philosophy."

Further, an internal critique using philosophy from within archaeology is emphasized. The problem with such hopes and declensions is that although philosophy may be treated as a disciplined manner of thinking and a way of knowing about knowing, is not a separate actor in any life world. It is not something that can be "brought to bear" in controlled and critical methods apart from the ambitions defined "internal" to any department of knowledge. Think here merely of the exercise in defining types of the afterlife that human consciousness has envisaged. This is the work of reflective thinking, and philosophy is merely an official name for such a process. This process is available to all of us, and is indeed necessary for all of us to become fully human. To this regard, both Wylie and Pinsky suggest that philosophy might be treated as an external source for critical analysis and valuable theoretical clarification, while both a generalized and totalizing conception of both history and the sociology of knowledge are expressed as "always present" and "inescapable." We might go even further, while allowing a pronounced critique of any set of texts that attempt to define what has passed, by following Merleau-Ponty (1964:108) in saying, "Philosophy is not a body of knowledge. It is the vigilance which does not let us forget the source of all knowledge."

The edited volume examines the interplay between philosophy of science and archaeology, detailing abuses on both sides. It is a history of misunderstanding, with both sets of practitioners unable or unwilling to try for an understanding of the other's motivations. "Philosophers" approached critical questioning and subject matter from a completely different perspective, often unaware of the archaeological questions that led to philosophical borrowings in the first place. This later blossomed into a prescriptive role that many archaeologists could not accept, territorially or intellectually. Although philosophers indicated that the ultimate arbiter of choice amongst the many alternatives to naive scientism should be cast in an archaeological mode, most practicing archaeologists ignored the texts altogether in favor of moving towards the hoped-for paradigmatic singularity. Philosophy of science would be another analytical tool for archaeologists to use indirectly, at certain specified nodes along the research process. Otherwise, it was to be excluded entirely. This reaction to "philosophy" as presented to archaeology demonstrated a lack of reflection amongst archaeologists. It is this same unreflective stance that we might encounter in our own lives, as per some of the forms that our personal and cultural memories take.

We have seen in the first chapter that we are all cast as archaeologists of ourselves, hence the relevance of a detailed discussion concerning how the official historians of the distant and unwritten past have decided to redefine our collective heritage. It was because of the perceived inability on the part of the philosophers to move to a space of "real knowledge" extant with the "true nature of science" that led to archaeologists' waning interest in any philosophical role. It seems that any philosophically-oriented discussion must be cast in terms not only comprehensible to archaeologists, but in terms that deal directly with their type of problems. This then becomes the major problem. The discussion ironically re-affirms the parochial quality of archaeology and those who practice it as being immune or insulated from critical analysis as provided by Wylie. It seems that many archaeologists perceive a figure like Wylie's contributions to be interesting, but then enable themselves to forget about them when they "go back to work." The "doing" of archaeology, whatever that may be, remains separate. We are left to wonder what changes archaeology can make to step into exploratory roles that keep such critiques constantly in mind. Apparently, the history of archaeology is one in which students have tried to isolate one tiny branch of quasi-philosophical thought and work under its protection, to the exclusion and subsequent ignorance of all other branches.

A discussion of the dual definitions and uses in archaeology of the concept of "efficient" explanations follows. "Efficiency" in the sciences denotes a formal property of any explanation, not necessarily whether the explanation describes an efficient behavior—because it is not the job of the logician to judge human efficiency (or inefficiency for that matter)—along the lines of something being an "efficient cause" of something else. This may be juxtaposed with other types of formal causality, such as both "necessary" versus "sufficient." The former must be there in order for something else to occur, but it by itself is not enough to get the job done. Hence, as an equation that bears certain relationships between its "causes" and "effects," its ultimate arbiter would seem a version of Occam's razor, where the simplest equation that "explains" all the variables or facts within any particular circumstance is probably the best one to use, if not the actual truth about the case. In light of this, the text critiques the idea of "efficiency" in explanations that use the term as a synonym for the set of human behaviors deemed most economical in the pursuit of imagined goals. This paradigm is familiar to all of us in the rationalized workplace, where the "one best way" is touted as not only being a reality, but being available to us to pursue without regard for any other contexts or situations. Much cultural ecological work in the human sciences partakes of this dubious framework, and much archaeological work borrows from ecological paradigms in that regard. This should not be surprising, as we have already seen with personal memory how convenient it is to forget certain actions and deeds that might make us feel less certain not only about our self-worth, but our effects on other people. In order to cast explanations as "efficient," archaeologists suggest that the idea that the "principle of least effort" controls human actions, and "all other things being equal" one can confidently posit the simplest explanation that takes care of the "facts." But such is not so simple as it may first seem.

The principle of least effort, as economy, may have its application in marketing the latest fuel-saving "economy" car, but not in logical explanation. Such a principle is too often and easily identifiable with "laziness," another cultural concept with dubious cross-cultural applicability. Also, we are seldom able to infer what "all things" are in any case, particularly archaeological, and hence for this reason—and even if we were able to provide a comprehensive list of relevant traits—we would not be able to tell whether or not they were indeed "equal." Thus the discussion concludes that while "efficient" explanations in their particular cases do not follow from the property of efficient explanations in science, the latter may have an appropriate role to play in archaeology.

We can then take a cue from Occam's razor and apply it to an archaeological test case where various evidences are explicated in the best manner possible, using a series of inferences. The simplest explanation may not be "the truth," or even closer to the truth than any other, but the logical apparatus used to approach the "shadow of truth" cannot be faulted as easily as uncritical ideas of what is "efficient" behavior. The only problem here is the inherent faith put into methods borrowed by archaeologists from the physical sciences, in this case, dating techniques such as the famous Carbon-14 radio-isotope. A series of seemingly well-founded premises based on archaeological analogues about a site's feature and its age and function were "disproved" by a late date. The moral for the text is not to necessarily trust even the best explanation using efficient analogical inference. Another moral is that the physical sciences provide "truth markers" that are accepted at face value because their self-same analogical and phenomenological properties are not well understood archaeologically, thus they are able to "correct" archaeological inference based on the student's personal archaeological experiences. This adherence to the truth claims of the physical sciences undermines any aspirations to a more interpretive or even critical truth claim shown by these authors to be unproblematic only in the archaeological realm.

Wylie then outlines the so-called diverse "interpretive dilemmas" in archaeology. Again, philosophy is seen as a "discipline." In this sense, it becomes akin to any other area of knowledge. Although Wylie herself rejects the implication that philosophy could or should become the "handmaiden of the sciences" (ibid:18), she blatantly overlooks the important distinction among philosophy as general ontological realm, epistemology, and philosophy of science. Yet it is striking that her description of the "strong empiricism" of archaeology as holding that any inference beyond the data themselves would be unsecured and perhaps even radical. But what are the data if not already that first radical movement into a linguistic sphere? Wylie makes no comment here, thereby jeopardizing the balance struck between "being" apparently real and that from which "being" springs. The social constructivist versus externally realist endeavor of Wylie could be fatal in undermining her critique of other kinds of knowledge.

Wylie anticipates an important point exemplified below by declaring that it is idealism about the relationship between ground and knowledge in a scientific stance that allows the illusion that the interpretive dilemma—in this guise that the present actions of the researcher must form at least part of the interpretation of any inferential action in the past or the present—can be escaped. Such a dialogue with critiques of science is seen as an extended attempt to outrun the interpretive pursuers of an uncritical and dogmatic materialist vision of the past and present. While our experience of scientific experimentalism is interactive—Wylie does not explain whether this means interpretive, dialogic, or another format—"normal" science workers can and do move beyond the box of thinking as it might stand today. That is, they do not have to exist as loci of the exacting and same power relations laid out as theory and imposed by method. The "essential tension" that exists between paradigms and their practitioners finds its parallel for Wylie in ethnoarchaeology, where direct experience and cultural knowledge of local descendants of those who presumably created the archaeological deposits in the first place allows us to test hypotheses about material remains, and change them to fit evidence garnered in the field.

Wylie, however, makes use of a distinction that seems problematic. The tensions allowing this sort of work, and process and "progress" in the sciences as well, seem to flow between the "more experiential and conceptual dimensions" and the paradigmatic impositions of the discipline. This distinction is a dubious one, for it may be more likely that whatever paradigm there is in place to guide the student, it is just as profound phenomenologically in the mind of the researcher, given that it also is written down in the study of science in general and is indicative of an intent in the respective literature and work of the discipline. Who reads the environment in ethnoarchaeology? What are the environmental, logistic, and material factors here? All such questions of interpretation still arise in a work that purports to do away with dilemmas that follow from them, but Wylie does not pursue the case further.

This problem is also our own. We may well claim to have negotiated the errors of our past, even to the point of stating that "this was my old self and I am now someone else," or that "this was another life lived." Yet we are also notoriously prone to repeat our past failures even if we see them in a new light, or perhaps even if they in fact stem from other origins than they may have in our pasts. Wylie's further distinction between "source side" and "subject side" modes of thinking in archaeology—and presumably elsewhere—is similarly in error if one continues to question along these lines. The terms used are also confusing: "source" sometimes appearing to denote the object reality of the source of interpretation, sometimes the human source of interpretation itself; where the "subject" is sometimes the subject of interpretation, sometimes the subject herself. Wylie declares, "This account of research practice avoids the untenably extreme formulations of both empiricist objectivism and Kuhnian or constructivist subjectivism" (Wylie:1989b:26). Perhaps this is an overstatement given that Wylie admits in a footnote that her formulation does nothing to resolve the interpretive dilemma if challenged by a so-called "global skeptic" (ibid:27) who might deny that "subject reality" knowledge is possible. We may well say to ourselves, especially in the face of probable death, that what we did and what we thought during life was ultimately only our opinion and others could just as well have ignored it, we are likely denying the influence we can and do have over other people when we attempt to coerce or cajole them into acting only in our best interests. What one can deny is the attempted authority claim that there exists either singularity in a dialogue with one another that assumes the position of a third eye or continued relevant existence without the subject as source at all, or at the very most without even human language as source and translator.

If Wylie unjustly duplicates some of the naivety apparent in archaeology through her manipulation of the "realities" surrounding interpretation, then it is fitting that the discussions in this edited volume continue with revealing just what goes on in the minds of the average American archaeologist regarding what constitutes theory, who does it, and why it exists in archaeology in the first place. To get at the "real" wisdom of the archaeologist, an ethnographic survey would do better than a textual one, or one in which just the "big names" would be consulted. This may be correct statistically, but such a method also guarantees nothing in the form of decisive or authoritative information. At best, this was an exercise in distinguishing the knowledge of the "personal" ideas of the academic archaeologist from the knowledge that gets into the scientific journals on the subjects of theory and method. In the end, however, the archaeologists construct the survey themselves, guiding the researcher's thoughts through their many rejections of the previous sampling attempts. Given that only 48 of 230 potential respondents were usable in the study, it would seem that archaeologists in the U.S.A. are either far too busy to waste time on such a study, or are just not interested. Yet it is striking to note that there may be a parallel between the exclusion of a "philosophical" role in archaeology as an encroachment of territory and the fact that the researcher was a philosopher that may have something to do with the poor response. Human beings, scientists, and non-scientists alike are usually wary of those who wish to expose potential hypocrisies or vices within our lives. It is enough that we ourselves must live with them, and if we must expose them we risk accentuating and exacerbating their presence in our memories. These things, too, live on after having lived. They are an ironic testament to the fact that nothing really quite dies within us, just as archaeology in general might well be seen as a massive attempt to reclaim our temporarily lost memories from the earth itself.

One archaeologist's response to the question "What is the difference between empirical and theoretical archaeology?" deserves replication here as it serves to point up that question and response dialogics do not necessarily elicit self-fulfilling prophecies, and seems an exception to the rule: "[The distinction] is misleading if it implies that the latter ['empirical archaeology'] does not employ (and perhaps even develop) some body of abstract concepts. But these might not be 'theoretical' in your sense; this is a significant issue for one who wants to know how 'theoretical archaeology' differs post-1960 from that previous. Explicitness and systematicization of abstract knowledge seems to be partly involved" (ibid:31). Most of the other published responses could have been written by the same person, paralleling the styles of most archaeological journal articles.

The volume also attempts to spell out the relationship that a Marxist-inspired dialectic might use to present "standard" archaeological enquiry. The usual expressions of the oppressed are utilized—truth is relative, science is ideologically driven, and there is no separation between mind and social world—and summarized as against archaeological "naiveties." The reason to couch these three important and generalizing statements about the nature of knowledge in Marxist terms is because the next step is to use these harbingers of "relativism" as weapons in an ideological class struggle, or even an knowledge-based class conflict. Therefore, dialectical "epistemology"—or a study of knowledge which is critical of itself—could not possibly claim a "relativist" stance—that is, one in which all claims to truth are akin to mere opinions—as it is itself driven by an ideological opportunism wishing to clear a space for its adherents. The text mentions the first thought in the previous sentence, but neglects the crucial second one. In so-called "logical" science, a profound disjunction between the world and the self is contrived. This contrivance anticipates a causal relationship between what is observed and inferential remarks about such observations. There is no convincing distinction made between what might constitute a dialectical epistemology and one for example, that is based upon hermeneutics or some other form of critical dialogue. Yet because this part of the analysis entertains a Marxist perspective, one might suggest that an adherent would have to use the word "dialectical." Obviously, there is much more to Marx's usage of the term than is revealed here. Such work in archaeology as the official source of our relationship to the past might be taken as a kind of call to arms, a kind of "take back our past" piece of rhetoric. Yet we well know that much of our past is seen today as worthless, and much of the rest contains a threat to us; we wish we had not done things in our lives, and thus we also wish that we had done other things instead.

A critical review of the first section of Wylie and Pinsky's edited volume rounds out the expressly "philosophical" contributions. The Marxist analysis comes under attack, yet not for the reasons given above: "One may take exception to this argument. Although the archaeologist's ideological position helps to determine the choice of problem, and the problem helps to determine the choice of archaeological data, there is an archaeological reality that exists independently of interpretation. This is made clear by the fact that two archaeologists are able to interpret the same burial either similarly or differently" (ibid:46). Suffice it to say that if there was an independent reality for interpretation of such, it would be irrelevant to any interpretation since it was not part of the interpretation in the first place. We do not have quite the same distance from the actions of our past selves. We, in some less mature guise perhaps, still did what we did. If there was such a world that could be seen as separate from our present self, it could not be called "archaeological," because to do so would be an interpretation, or already is one. Similarly, a "site" is not a "natural" feature. It exists because we have identified it as a site, regardless of what else it might be. It is the "site" that is of archaeological, and hence of interpretive, import. The phenomenally unknowable world is not made any clearer by the idea that two archaeologists can witness it differently or similarly. How can we tell what is the same here if two or two hundred different interpretations arise? They do not arise from the "same" thing, then are given over to a diversity of erroneous interpretations. Interpretations arise because of human perception. Even before perception begins, we may well experience the inertia of "seeing what we want to see," or "to see or not to see," and hence our assumptions color all observation in a linguistic form before we even say something, let alone excavation and the recognition of a "site."

Our memories hold the same relation to us as individuals. They too exist in "sites" within the architecture of the brain, and these may even be identified by neuro-scientific procedures. The idea that there is an underlying "sameness" allowing human perception to fly tangentially away from a non-human reality is questionable at best. Here, the structure of presumed reality is only given by archaeological interpretation, and no one can draw an absolute line between the labels "pile of bones," "pile of human bones," and "burial"—or rather, one can draw a line, but claiming a non-arbitrary division once it is drawn is disingenuous.

Archaeologists are ready and able to believe in the cultural relativism of an ethnologically supported set of diverse versions of truth from around the world but, curiously, they cannot extend this "liberal attitude" to their own domain. This "inability to recognize "possible worlds" in prehistory" contributes to the stagnation of archaeological research. The text relates a humorous example of such an irony: "Few prehistorians believe that a single archaeological culture produces thirty different types of ceramics having the same function. However, place them in an ethnographic situation and not only will they recognize such diversity, but they will compete to procure examples of each type for their collections!" (ibid:47).

An interesting experiment with the texts and two readers is documented in the Conclusion (ibid:48). The analyses discussed above were read by both a social anthropologist and a philosopher, with strong criticisms attached, none of which was reproduced above. Disciplinary boundedness was seen as a major constraint in the set. This led to an insularity regarding concepts and ideas. The anthropologist could not believe that some archaeologists found an identity relation between material culture and human ideas, especially by virtue of extended analogies. The philosopher found that the relevant authorities that would make valuable extension to the discussions were not mentioned—presumably out of ignorance. If we and the archaeologists both hope to move in the directions advocated by the texts in question, then this would seem a dubious beginning.

The idea of history in the general sense is invoked in the next section of this crucial volume. History is not seen as disciplinary in the hegemonic sense, but "only" in the sense that it constrains our every action and thought through the processes of an historical consciousness. The major problem with the discussions here is that history is seen as a totalizing movement, one in which the further "back" one goes in time, the more distance one must infer to make difference valid. More importantly, but following from this in part, is the idea that a continuous history with the ability to be appropriated by us is still tenable. The second point seems to be in direct contradiction to the first. How can we make the connection if the connection disappears on the horizon, traveling away from us at the breakneck speed of a turn and run whiplash? In a fundamental manner, this bond is sundered by the discussion that follows.

Perhaps we should not be calling this kind of conversation a "volume" at all. Are all of our memories—what we have been and done as a person as well as what we have seen others do, as a local witness to a larger human history—in good order and can we put our fullest trust in them True, these appeared to be bound as books are: they are contained within a single crania. Yet when we read our minds, they fly apart in our metaphoric hands, as if their binding had aged beyond the ability to hold the entirety of our life's experience together. This in itself might be seen as a harbinger of our own actual loss of memory as we ourselves age. The question "How could I have forgotten such a thing?" eventually becomes forgotten itself. At this point, the muteness which is itself a sentinel of death looms near. A wonder that any publisher could have found covers strong enough to contain these internal conflicts. The attempted radicalisation of priorities is consistently undermined and re-oriented by the reactionary hold-overs from what wishes to be called a "previous" era. Thus politics is undercut by memory, rejection of truth claims collapses under other external modes which use just such claims. An exercise in "schizophrenia" occupies this "volume" as its *raison d'etre*. The struggle that occupies center stage is already defined as a denouement within the archaeological theatre of reconstructed histories.

Our memory of ourselves is always under revision, as we saw early on, and thus is always temporary and transitional, no different from the cultures of the past which ended as littering the planet with forgotten objects and equally mortal deeds. Relations of archaeo-historic events, or of historical events with archaeological import, is well presented and documented in detail. A reading of discourse, its potential shifts, and its regulation of and from its sources is relevant here. In general, however, the type of history evidenced would seem little more than case studies occupying previously-empty historical space. Indeed, it is left to the third section of the edited volume to deal with that space in an ideological manner.

The prehistory to the first British Ancient Monuments Protection Act (of 1882) is of interest in that there seems some striking parallels with the contemporary archaeological scene. Today, archaeology is constantly involved in conservational or ethical disputes, legalities, and the politics associated with these murky waters. It is not clear for example, that there is any difference between what is characterized as preservationist tendencies in Victorian England, the romanticizing nationalisms and craving for a "people's" folklore, and the state of much archaeological motivation today (ibid:60). Historicism and Romanticism may go hand in hand, shaping the contemporary strategy of "saving that which is of value." How value is determined, in other words, is most likely a political function informed by these two themes. If it is, then how far has prehistory come as a political appendage or set of ideological acts? This critique tells us "not very far." The style of historical exposition is clearly set in historical hermeneutics, where the context of the past is to be recaptured with an aspiration to "truth" through both atmosphere and empathy. As such it works well, but probably only does so not because of a standard interpretive "tool." Instead, it "works" as a good story because it tells us about our present situation in the form of a direct allegorical play. How often do we reminisce about our individual pasts in the same way? We might wish to present to our children a lesson in life, or to our students an exemplar of a theoretical point, or to a would-be lover a humorous or mischievous escapade, the kind of thing that lets the intimate other know that we are human like themselves. We then can be trusted with intimacy itself.

A famous case in point is the history of Stonehenge studies. This rewrites the history of commentary upon Stonehenge from c. 1150 A.D. to the present through an appeal to the totalizing history of a progressive science. If we believe that other ages may have used incipient scientifically correct archaeological techniques in their description of Britain's most famous monument then this demonstrates an inherent evolutionary progress towards modern science, one which even embodies the same basic questions and dichotomous equations. Such a discussion re-enforces conservative and scientistic modes of being within history and the language of history. Such language is hardly "oracular" in any other sense than it foreshadows a successive history, in turn held in thrall by contemporary politics. Thus it takes the form of a reading of texts back into the past with a currency that always had the potential of being out of place which actual history. It is the same argument and method used when we naively declare that our modern science is 2500 years old, that what we do now was also present in the Greek study of knowledge, and that what we know now is foreshadowed and even allowed by the Greek understanding of humanity as a form of unique but unquiet being. All of this is a partial truth, but one that must be well-situated in the shadow of the cultural limits of ancient science. It questioned the nature of the cosmos, but never the order of its own society. Allowing our past to become the prophecy of our future is a risky business indeed.

The American philosopher Valerie Pinsky's review of these discussions is of interest because she casts them in the light of the dichotomous dilemma between the interpretivist's historical relativism and the historian's objective treatment of the past as artifact. The first is accomplished by bringing together: a) the understanding of history as a form of the present, and b) that of the understanding of past as also with us in the present can serve a specific ideology. Either way, it is impossible to know the past, unless empathy is employed as a calculated naivety. Do we really feel the way our ancestors felt? Do we even know what it was like to live when they did? Contrived television melodramas like "Colonial House" aside, it is one thing to mimic the techniques of historical life and production, including subsistence and diet, but quite another to conjure from the innumerable graves of once-sentient humanity the feelings and beliefs of our predecessors. On the other hand, the objectification of history as merely that which is "past" is also untenable. We seem to be left with the unsatisfactory idea that the history of archaeology, or the archaeology of memory, can be told with integrity from within. Hopefully such will not take the form of an attempt to remain "within" history, as Pinsky labels this as a possible "internalist" perspective. We are always in history of course, but is that history enabled as a process of becoming, or is it merely a weight against any creative potential for being something other than we were? If one utilizes the "method" involved in the ideological appropriation of history, then perhaps we may at least be honest and sincerely consistent with ourselves, while not necessarily agreeing with the ideologies we may find embedded within the sediments of our consciousness.

Wylie begins her introduction to the third and final section of this edited volume: "The essays in this section mark a significant break with all earlier traditions of reflection on archaeological practice" (ibid:93). Each of the three articles in the section is given over to a provoking socio-political critique. Each has an ideological axe to grind. For the first time, with the exception of some possible problems to be discussed below, there may be an actual cognizance of a foreseen horizon which consists of a fundamentally different manner of knowledge acquisition and communication in both archaeology proper and any personal excavation of our newly-recalled selves.

Scientific archaeology as an imperialist entity is explored within the context of the popular non-archaeologically and non-academically trained interpretation of New England "beehive" structures in opposition to their virtual invisibility in the academic literature. It should be noted that even the architecturally- and archaeologically-inspired "pure" description of these structures could be considered imperialist under her own critique (ibid:98). What is most interesting about this piece is that it does not itself provide an interpretation, leaving the reader in search of the "answer" to this wonderful mystery created by the tensions between two mythological camps, each entrenched in their authority and "facts." The text simply says enigmatically, "Additional research is inevitably needed" (ibid:102). Much of what we can recall of our lives, fading with age in the same way as does the larger history around us, remains open to "further research." Much of what we have done in our lives has had consequences that do not allow us to quite close the door upon them. They linger, not unlike the smell of cadaverous death, long after the body itself is removed from the scene. Do we even desire to commit to "further research" of such events and their implications? The idiom "let sleeping dogs lie" does not, of course, refer to dogs.

The final review of the third section of Wylie and Pinsky's volume takes a mild stance, but warns that archaeology itself must not take lightly the socio-political critique as represented therein. It outlines four possible receptions, from internalizing such a critique as one of many archaeological tools akin to "…taphonomy, phytoliths and geochemistry…" (ibid:137); to the "arealizing" of it, with some parts of archaeology immune to critique while others more circumspect with regard to potential critics; to the de-archaeologizing of socio-political critique by placing it into another science; or even more reactionary, to practice the exclusion of such a critique from the entire body of all the sciences. None of these responses is satisfactory because they breathe the naive and dangerous idea that we as persons are aloof to social circumstances not reflected in our own immediacy—if it does not affect us, we need not be concerned with it. We can easily foster the same diffidence with our memories, as well as with the edgy horizon of our future inexistence. The bold motto, "Seize the day," might well remind us that we must also "Look before we leap." How far ahead we look depends perhaps on our respective existential tastes. Even so, we feel we cannot live for the day alone, especially if there are others to whom we bear existential responsibilities—children, loved ones, aging parents. The collective future of humanity must be included within this list of intimates lest the very possibility of intimate community perish.

The final contribution to this archaeological discussion is the most vocal and most radical in the volume. It begins with a construction of a kind of bad conscience. Suffice it to say that this is the most trenchant and shocking critique of archaeology as a discipline and as a general metaphoric practice to this point in time. Not that any of the points it makes are radical in and of themselves—that archaeology commodifies the past, that it supports the capitalist oppression of global humanity, that it creates new fetishes for wealthy or otherwise privileged persons to consume, that archaeologists themselves are knowing instruments of this imperialism, and that archaeology is a conservative weapon against all potential forces of global change, to name a few—it is just that it is rare if not unique to see them openly and unabashedly declared in an academic setting. It states at one point in its critique of scientism in archaeology that "any attempt to reduce archaeology to the science of the artefact would entail silence" (ibid:110). One could go even further, because silence is also perhaps a "too" linguistic concept. It rather might entail death.

There are some very Nietzschean overtones to such an argument. One example can suffice. The text suggests making "writerly" museums the norm—where the visitors arrange the exhibits and interpret them. This idea works to make the text serious by at first laughing at it. Sardonic humor, usually ill-natured, might be employed in order to allow the meaning of the past to reach us in a manner associated with the edgy reproach of all sarcasm. Power relations are the guiding principle of this effort and it may be seen as producing the first critique of archaeology in the omniscient light of the schema of power, knowledge, resistance, and desire. This final analysis makes ample use of the death of the author. Perhaps it is just beguiling enough to wish us to think that we bear the responsibility for knowing history in this way or that. Such a critique has brought off a consistent and violent movement that will have to be reckoned with in any future.

The sense that we have a future as long as we know not the fact of our future—we live on but we do not know how long we will live—is brought into the harshest light by those of our fellow humans who apparently take their future into their own hands by killing themselves. The depersonalization of suicide is the second major source of being able to live on after living, as it allows those who are left behind to continue to live in the face of what is essentially the same knowledge as that possessed by those who have elected not to live on. Yes, it is certain that some lives have a much higher quality of happiness, comfort, and access to resources than others. Indeed, most human lives are by our standards insufferable. It is perhaps our greatest social hypocrisy that we maintain the political pretense that these other humans "like the way they live" in the same way that we like our lifestyles. Akin to statements regarding the plight of the homeless in wealthy societies—they must prefer to live "like that"—we practice a global denial of the human condition, crossing the metaphorical street writ large when the homeless or impoverished come into view.

In a social experiment motivated by profit, my hometown constructed affordable housing for all of its homeless population. The West Coast has a climate that draws marginal persons from across the country. It was found that there were indeed a few homeless people—middle-aged men with dual diagnoses, both drug-addicted and mentally ill—who refused this opportunity, simply because they did not wish to live by any normative structure and stricture whatsoever. The city did not force them to comply. Yet the vast majority of homeless persons immediately accepted the accommodation and its rather loose regulations, with the result of the downtown being a more placid place. The fact that this seeming philanthropy was accomplished because the city and its entrepreneurs did not want the tourist trade to be affected by marginal persons interrupting the usual beauties of the surrounding setting cannot be ignored, but it also should not be disdained. Similarly, the implication of a suicide, especially of someone close to us, may neither be ignored nor disdained. The suicide accomplished rids the world of someone who, at least in their own mind, felt they were marginal. They could not go on living after living out what their life was so far. The future appeared as bleak as did the past. The norms of what was to come looked identical to the norms of what had gone before. Those who took up a new residence off the streets accepted new norms because the opportunity was there. Is there a similar kind of opportunity available for those contemplating their own demise? Or do those who commit suicide do so because they cannot in any context accede to the norms society wishes to set down for them?

The founder of sociology, Emile Durkheim, studied this problem in detail. Yet he went about it by asking if there were not patterns to suicides that had the same character as those found in more "natural" events such as mortality rates. His findings are still relevant today, and the statistical analysis he used still holds up in the regions from which he collected archival data. That is, these cultural areas still exhibit similar rates and types of suicide as they did a century ago.

How does Durkheim demonstrate his thesis through the use of social statistics, specifically those relating to suicide? By using some decades of European data culled from different regions, he suggests not only a set of variables which are relevant to the likelihood of persons socially constructed in their life-chances by these variables of committing suicide, but also a model of types of suicide and their character, as well as the kinds of societies where these types would likely predominate. The key construct variables were strong obligations to either an extant and concentrated community and weak obligations to a diffuse or even non-existent community, or correspondingly, the relative strength or weakness of sense of self over against society, i.e., the idea of individuality:

Table 1 Categories of social suicide and their predominant rates regionally.

relative presence or absence of construct variable:	+ community	- community
+ individuality	"fatalistic" suicide (empty set)	egoistic suicide (North America)
- individuality	altruistic suicide (traditional societies)	anomic suicide (Europe)

One would surmise, on the face of it, that where there existed a strong sense of both oneself and the others to whom one is obligated, suicide would be rare or absent. Indeed, Durkheim mentions the possibility of this category only in a footnote. We can call these potential events, however Ibsen-like they may appear to be, "fatalistic." The person would presumably feel the weight of too many conflicting obligations. If we look at it in a slightly different manner, such a person might be quite liable to commit suicide, but cases which truly fit this category still seem to be rare. It is likely that most persons who find themselves striving for self-fulfillment in a society that resents the intrusion of the self-concept into a more collective sense of community eventually either acquiesce to the demands of the others or leave their communities entirely. The modern cityscape is full of such persons, following their dreams but at the same time working to engender often makeshift and transient communities of others like themselves. A standard recent example of this social trend may be found from the 1960s onwards as gay Americans left their regions of birth and migrated to California, only to find that once there, all they indeed shared with the potential community partners was their sexual orientation.

It is perhaps more of a challenge to parse the "fatalistic" and the egoistic, or yet even the altruistic categories, as we generally do not have access to the interiors of such persons who self-sacrifice in this manner. Another sociological study found that about only twelve percent of suicides leave notes. As this study was done in the United States, almost all of them were directed towards the ironic preservation of the ideal of self through the immolation of the actual self, in other words, to a kind of egoism. This category, where we expect to find those who are disenchanted with the world or feel that they themselves are too good for the world and those others who inhabit it, kill themselves almost out of spite or the seeking of revenge. There may well be much resentment involved in the egoistic category, and yet, because Durkheim refrains from judging these cases as egotistical, following Rousseau's original distinction between the care of the self through egoism and the narcissism associated with the egotist, we are left to wonder if the ultimate form of "care" is self-preservation as only a specific set of memories that find their resonant residence in those that live on. Such a memory is engraved in our minds, especially due to the radicality of the act. It is also well known, however, that those who are left behind also bear some resentment to the one who has departed in such a fashion, and this once again presents to the analytic the edginess of the egoistic category. The self comes first and foremost, and the potential suffering of others is quite secondary. It is not surprising to find that this type is predominant in the more individually-oriented and immigrant societies of North America.

In sharp contrast to the egoist, intent on representing the self as sacrosanct and untouchable in the most radical manner, collective societies, especially those that we saw Durkheim called "mechanical," find a much more traditional meaning in the idea of self-sacrifice, as we shall see shortly. That is, one sacrifices oneself on behalf of the group. The continued existence of the community takes utter and absolute precedence over the needs or desires of any person within it. We may imagine that the apparent nobility of all persons in this category from the very beginning of the social contract and humanity's presence on the earth has played a not-unimportant role in the reproduction of human society, from the confrontations with wild animals to the blithe and obliterative acts that forestall nature's indomitable forces. Yet we also know that altruism is a relative thing, and the perpetrators of acts of violence—terrorism, organized warfare, espionage, etc.—also act to preserve their community over against others. This would include those who kill themselves in order to kill others who are strangers to their own society. So this category, too, has an edginess about it, even though its face value suggests something more impressive and ethical than that found in the acts of the egoist.

The category that Durkheim was most interested in, however, was that of the "anomic." This term, invented by Durkheim to reference "anomie," or alienation, lack of structure, and normlessness, appeared to fit the European scene extremely well. During the fin de siècle period, there was an increasing loss of interest in both the community and the self. It is one thing to imagine that the world at large holds no place for myself because I am special and that this goes unrecognized, or may even be treated with injustice, or, in its obverse, to hold the claim that the world must be altered in order for a collective entity to survive. It is yet another thing, however, to suggests that no world that either self or society could create would be worth living in. The increasing absence of intimate communities in modern capitalistic societies is well known, and this trend has continued apace in Europe since Durkheim's day. An extreme but altogether common case concerning one dying alone appeared in the German news some years ago. A man, living alone, had apparently stopped paying his utilities and rent bills for the apartment which he inhabited. After three months or so the management asked the police to enter the suite, and to their astonishment, they found that the only audience the television had was a grinning skeleton, remote control still in its grasp. The man had been dead for six years, and the automatic debiting of his account had until recently continued to pay his bills from beyond the grave, as it were.

There is a sudden sociological exercise of self-recognition imbedded in all such tales. How long would it take for you to be found if you had died suddenly, and who would be the person most likely to discover you? If the response includes "more than a few days" and "professionals," you are likely to understand anomie better than some. With the other three forms of suicide there is a sense of grand tension between sets of conflicting norms, but with the anomic variety, there is a sense that norms themselves do not exist. As we are preeminently a social animal driven by adherence to norms and rules, says Durkheim, the absence of both suggests that we ourselves are non-existent, and thus it is but a small step to complete the operation of removal of this once-living human and social being from the now-barren world.

Alienation means something quite different in Durkheim than it does for Marx, for instance, who saw it as a confluence of four different situations arising from what the latter called "wage-slavery" and the relationship of the worker to the means of production, which is that he did not own it. For the former, alienation is felt as a subjectivity, even though it too may be considered as social fact. It is the sum of at least seven other variables, and its relative presence or absence, depending in turn on the more measurable or observable presences or absences of these others, is an explanatory factor in the probability that individuals of a certain structural type will or will not kill themselves. Successive generations of sociologists have added to Durkheim's original list, but the most salient factors appear in table six. For our purposes, we have limited the statistical analysis to the simplest form of the probable, "more or less likely." The pattern for Durkheim was clear. As stated above, he found that the presence of variables which denoted strength or weakness of social bonds—community both in general and amongst intimates—and their corresponding relative presence or absence of obligation and responsibility to these others tells the tale:

Table 2 Structural variables influencing the life-chances of suicide of persons over the life course as defined by their categorical implications. *Other religions were neutral; ** includes social class of parents; *** for modern purposes, any relationship that has lasted longer than a year; **** not one of Durkheim's variables.

Structural Variables:	greater likelihood of suicide	lesser likelihood of suicide
gender	male	female
religion*	Protestant	Catholic
social class**	professional or middle class	working class or proletarian
"marriage"***	unmarried	married
age	16–39	40 plus
networks or community	absent or diffuse	present and intimate
ethnicity or "race"****	"white"	non-white

All of the factors that imply that one has "settled down" and has an increasing amount of normative responsibilities—to spouse, children, even to work or extended families—were not only measurable but had face validity. The fact that, especially in Durkheim's time, regions of Europe which were predominantly Catholic represented more intimate and extended communities and families with their concurrent obligations on the individual explained much. As will be detailed in Chapter Five, it was the rise of our modern form of economic system, capitalism, that fostered the new and very much Protestant belief that the destiny of the individual was to be considered paramount. That egoistic suicide continues to be the type practiced in more individuated societies underscores this difference. The rise of Protestantism in its individuating forms—contrast the Calvinist with the traditional Anabaptist, for instance—also was specific to cultural regions where "white" persons were to be found, the areas of Northern Europe. In agrarian societies—India, China, etc.—a more communitarian ethos prevailed, while in traditional pre-agrarian social formations such as pastoralism and horticulture—Central Asia and

East Africa versus sub-Saharan West Africa, respectively—the altruistic form held a monopoly on such acts. As mercantilism replaced agrarianism in Northern Europe, followed by urbanization and then colonial immigration, suicide rates diverged markedly from the Mediterranean regions. The rise of the middle classes, with their individuated consciousness of not merely material success but also, and perhaps originally, borne on the notion that their relationship with the Protestant God was a personal one, also told true for Durkheim's analysis. That one of the most famous studies in the social sciences, and the first to use quantitative methods in any large and systematic manner, could be seen as a reaction to the social disintegration which had plagued Europe, and especially France, over the preceding century, does not obviate its contemporary relevance. Nor have the numbers changed all that much in the century succeeding Durkheim. It is still far more likely, given the variables listed, that certain types of persons will commit suicide than others. Needless to say, the vast majority of persons in any category find a way to adapt to the stressors of life, but it would be interesting to follow persons designated in the middle column of Table Two, those with supposedly higher chances of suicide, in order to see what their lives are like and how they have engendered enough of the other variables over which one has some control—community vs. age, for instance. That Durkheim felt the necessity for the presence of variables implying or creating social solidarity is plain, given that one could argue that the persons in such a study were but microcosms of a larger and more structural implication that the personal suicide was not merely a metaphor for the suicide of society, but a reflection of it.

This analysis of what is usually cast as an intimate and psychological act was revolutionary in our understanding of how society not only imposes its version of life upon us, but also its version of death. Yet if we take Durkheim seriously, it allows us to depersonalize such apparently private acts and bring them once again into the whole cloth of cultural context. It gives us necessary perspective, indeed, in this case the most necessary one, as we are still living on the edge of complete and collective mass suicide, as if the global society were some kind of cult. In fact, the mass suicides that have become notorious over the past decades occurred precisely because those who joined them had lost all sense of social perspective. Think of Jonestown, Heaven's Gate, and the Solar Temple cults—the latter two associated with beliefs that extra-terrestrial beings were going to "pick up" the spirits of those who had killed themselves—and we quickly get the picture. It is well known that cults—a term which used sociologically merely means a religious group too small and irregular to be called a church—canvas their membership from persons disaffected with the normative society. They are suffering, in other words, from precisely what Durkheim understood as one of the chief causes of suicide: anomie, or normlessness. They have neither belief in the self nor in society; they disdain the idea of living on as individuals; they also shun the suggestion that they could live on as a member of a culture. This depressing situation is one which is ripe for the "salvation" represented by a new, abnormative belief. Yet it is not the beliefs per se that animate the cult recruit, but the promise of instant community. Those who are more connected to their lives and their cultures join churches, not cults, and those who are the most connected to modern society through work, family, friends, and indeed, consumer spending habits and wealth, tend not to join any other group at all, religious or no.

So it behooves us in the most profound manner to come to the fullest understanding of what social forces drive persons to feel alienated, for it is personal alienation that is the surest sign that life is hanging in the balance. The cult of the commodity, or the pursuit of wealth, or the hoarding of resources does have the potential to force a global suicide upon us all. If we are serious about living on after living, if we are to consider the afterlife in its proper place, whatever its character may be, then we must first address the issues that exist in this life and this world that keep human beings from thinking that their lives are worth living, and that the history of the species is best thought of as courageous and inherently worthwhile in its continuation. Both the critical study of our collective past as a memory that can once again be shared by not only the descendants of those who lived in archaeologically-revealed cultures and civilizations, but can be, for the first time, shared as a collective memory of the human birthright, as well as the threat of suicide as a reflection of a society that alienates its members from itself and from each other, allows us the dual perspective necessary for human life.

We have seen that we are ultimately a forward-thinking species. The evidence of this includes the perhaps ironic cultivation of the idea of the afterlife. We will with the strongest possible desire and emotion, and engage with the keenest and most assiduous intellect, the idea that our consciousness should live on in some way. Preparing for this eventuality—for after all, we will all encounter an afterlife of some kind, we will get there from here—cannot include the premature short-circuiting of what we know humanity consists of in this life. Every major form of the afterlife examined in the previous pages reminds us that what we do in this life will affect our future. Unevaluated return means that we come back to the world as it was when we left it. What kind of world, then, did we leave? What state was it in? Would we wish to return to it as it was? Evaluated return means that we come back in a form befitting our acts in the previous life. Do we really wish to return as a much more limited species, or in a lower social location in a hierarchical society—meaning we would have that much less influence, but this is of course the whole point, given that our previous life's influence on others and society as a whole was mostly negative—and then suffer such consequences as we might deserve? Evaluated continuation means that we move on to some other world, but do we wish to live in the comfort of the love of our kindred and of a God, or do we wish to suffer the indemnities of the shadowy underworld where hope is lost? Unevaluated continuation means that we leave the world to others who will either suffer for our past actions in it, or will benefit from all of the good works we strived over a lifetime for. Which would we rather choose: the perhaps eternal memories that we could have done much more and did not, or the satisfaction and fulfillment that come from living to the best of our abilities and helping others do the same? With this form of the afterlife, there is no going back to right the wrongs of our earthly life, and presumably this new form of consciousness, whatever it might be, has not the power to act from afar, wherever that may be.

Finally, and perhaps most radically, if the afterlife means oblivion, the total and fatal loss of all human consciousness, and the return to the cosmos of the elements of which we are made, then one must live life ethically all the more. We might well argue that it is this fifth form of the afterlife that tells us that nothing matters, but here we would be in error. This most recent idea concerning the fate of mortal humanity contains within it our greatest challenge. If there is no ultimate reward or punishment for our acts in life and no memory of them to guide us further, if there is no return to try again in the world we know and love, then we are faced with the finite knowledge that it is all or nothing. Only the most cynical person who has been relieved of the responsibility of social conscience would stake his claim on the nihilistic version of nothingness, and thus be capable of all and any acts, no matter how outrageous. Though they are rare, that these persons exist is a reminder to the rest of us that life is all the more sacred if it is the only one.

Epilogue: The Death of Death

A Few Words on Indefinite Life

We have spoken of human consciousness in the terms that we have come to know from our history thus far. Yet we are on the very cusp of revolutionary changes to this consciousness that might well nullify the idea of the afterlife itself. I speak here about the developments in three areas of non-human consciousness that stand to alter forever the course of what human beings are, know, and can know about the cosmos and ourselves. There are three such developments hanging just within the horizon of our current self-understanding and technological prostheses. They are: artificial intelligence, cybernetic prosthesis, and extraterrestrial intelligence. We can say a few words about each in turn, and then dwell for a moment on their apparent implications for humanity.

I often suggest to my students that theirs may well be the last generation to die a natural human death. That is, aside from accidents, crimes, warfare, and diseases, the breakdown of the body due to organic aging processes might be in its twilight. Indeed, it is a great stretch of the human imagination to envisage the eradication of all forms of human death, especially that which we commit against one another through premeditation, but it is not so great a leap to think that both organic and cybernetic prostheses—the first through stem cell replacement research and the second through nano-technology and the like—would see a drop even in the accidental death and disease categories. Freud famously referred to modern humans as the "prosthetic gods," but all of human history has been made possible in large part by our resourceful manipulation of the natural environment, beginning with the first tools of stone and other materials plentiful and at hand on the savannahs of eastern Africa. Correspondingly, we have reached a point in human cultural evolution where our now-youthful generation's children may be able to live indefinitely. Stem cell research itself must ethically be limited to those who suffer from chronic and painful diseases or accident victims or victims of crime. Replacement body parts that are necessary for life to continue can be reasonably and even morally sought. It is another question if we begin to desire aesthetically "superior" parts to refashion our bodies to suit the commercial or even intellectual preferences of the day. The spectre of Huxley's *Brave New World* and its genetically manufactured hierarchies of humanity haunts all radical attempts at organic prosthesis. There is also the problem of the division of labor. How many so-called super-intellectual persons would be fulfilled by running a backhoe, or being a plumber? The concert pianist who also fits gas valves might be a possible figure, but for now, not a plausible one.

This is where the second form of new consciousness comes on the scene. Indeed, it interfaces with the first through cybernetic prostheses. There already is a kind of quasi-telepathic helmet used by victims of multiple sclerosis and similar diseases that is able to "read" certain electro-chemical signals in the brain and translate them into commands such as "Open the door" or "Turn on the light." An infra-red beam is used to initiate the action at a distance once the helmet has ascertained the person's thoughts. This technology is still experimental and is very limited, but it represents the trend of non-invasive cybernetic prosthesis that will only continue. Scientists in both Britain and the USA have inserted micro-chip technologies into their limbs to help transfer muscle signals across injured gaps from body part to body part, or interpret muscle motions, such as the flexing of one's arm or clenching of one's wrist, to perform similar functions as the aforementioned helmet.

But aside from all of these ventures, artificial intelligence proper has almost come of age. In Japan, nano-therapies can be syringed into the body to fight diseases, or record processes within the interior of organs, or yet aid in the production of certain enzymes and proteins. These machines are so small that they remind one of none other than the angels on the head of a pin, that stereotypical characterization of scholastic philosophy. The grand idea behind such miniscule robotics is that they will eventually be able to fight cancer cells on the front lines, grappling with them and destroying them as if in hand-to-hand combat. The enormous saving of energies and resources within the rest of the still-healthy body cannot be underestimated. No more chemotherapy or radiation sickness. More trivially, no more debates about the medical use of marijuana. It is but a small step from these advances to intelligent machines that can help our natural immune defenses in policing activities of dangerous invaders in the bloodstream, liver, lungs, etc. Between organic and cybernetic prosthesis, and actual autonomous artificial intelligence, the future of humanity, though altered, begins to look far less mortal.

Artificial intelligence also addresses the very human problem of the division of labor. Honda's series of robots—fittingly nicknamed "Asimo" after the famous American scientist and science fiction author, Isaac Asimov—not only sport extended vocabularies but also perform routine domestic functions like vacuuming the rugs or mowing the lawn. Though perhaps a petty use of advanced technology, these machines are part of a package, a holistic wave of robotics that attempts to take on any task which humans are disinclined to perform. The problem of artificial intelligence is also one that Huxley would have recognized. If the robots become sentient—either by their own evolution from prior programming or through our calculated efforts to produce a new form of conscious life—it would be unethical to demand of them the trivial in the same manner as we would ideally disdain it ourselves. Still, the labors of the day need to be accomplished somehow. Should we then construct "races" of robots of different capacities, or castes of worker robots that are programmed to "love their jobs" in the cheerful way that the American sociologist and political thinker, C. Wright Mills, jeered at our then-nascent service sector? And if such technology remains a commodity, who amongst us will be able to afford it over the short and long terms? Do we replicate with the new forms of consciousness the old forms of social organization?

I think that we can do better than this. Indeed, it will be a healthy challenge to humanity to have other forms of intelligent life, with correspondingly different perspectives on the world, living side by side with us. These new forms will not necessarily be loyal to human emotions, moralities, or other beliefs and desires. Unlike the image of God which many religious narratives state that we were made in, we should perhaps shy away from playing God by constructing new life in our own image, let alone to our wishes. The attentiveness to each of us as an individual, unique, yet with a conscience that always must in turn lend itself to the greater good might well be translated by the robots or other machines to a greater self-understanding from which we can gain a valuable new self-perception. We have long thought of ourselves as the "as-ness" of the divine. By this I mean that the finite human being is made only in the likeness of God, which is what the term "image" implied when these ideas were first written down. An "image" is not the real thing, but a copy, just as we might have a photo-reproduction of a great work of art in our homes, the original of which we could never afford—nor, perhaps, would we wish to own such an artifact in private given that it is part of our shared human heritage. Our finite image of the infinite, humans as akin to the gods but not actually within the envelope of the divine, nor being equal or in identity with God or the cosmos, is what is implied by the idea of "as-ness." This may be juxtaposed with "is-ness." The hope of the afterlife is that it consists of the hypostasized "as-ness," that is, that the afterlife turns as-ness into is-ness. Many conceptions of the afterlife, as we have seen, have the aspiration of communion with what is greater than ourselves. The likeness of the image of the gods daunts us, and perhaps we are even resentful of our smaller and less valuable copy of something infinitely more important and significant in the cosmic order. The alchemy of the afterlife transmutes us from the lead of mortality to immortal gold, thus making our value the same as God's. If the mythic project of projects is the heroic self of selves, then the hope of the afterlife is the hypostasized aspiration of all ethics.

The prosthetic godhead of hypothetical alien species has long been a fetish in popular culture, almost from the very beginning of the post-war "UFO era." Recently, serious scientific searches have gotten underway, buoyed by the use of new technologies, and it is common to hear in media reports from these sites that expectations are high that we will make undeniable and empirical public contact with such beings—whatever they may be—within a generation or so. This at first seems far-fetched, but the amount of the galaxy that can be scanned for possible signals, as well as the quantity of star clusters we can ourselves send signals to, has been geometrically expanded in a few short years. The entire night sky is the goal of the new Allen Observatory in Oregon, where eventually some 400 radio telescopes will be built and interconnected. The deepest and widest scans will then be possible, to the very origins of this apparent version of the universe, to the very edges of what it appears to be. The limitation of the speed of light and interstellar differences seem to be the only physical limits to this kind of endeavor. This said, extra-solar planets—those not in our solar system—abound quite near to us. An earth-like world was discovered a mere twenty light years from here a few months ago, and next year a new satellite will be launched to search specifically for such worlds, which statistical extrapolation suggests will constitute a significant percentage of alien solar systems. This is not to say that intelligent life in the galaxy must correspond to our human imagination or our aesthetics, but that our technology is designed, for now, to search for that relatively narrow band of life with which we are most familiar. It is interesting that it is private enterprise that has taken the lead on this count. Such intelligence, if discovered—and if we can, in fact, communicate with it using our mathematics and physics which we hope to be universal in nature such that "they" would also understand—would be unlike anything we have known. This kind of event, an objective and public extraterrestrial contact—likely first occurring in a similar manner as in the romantic Hollywood film of the same name—would be perhaps the greatest event in the history of humanity.

All three new forms of consciousness, two immediately on the human horizon and for all we know the third lingering just over it, entail a vast extension of both human perception and perspective. They also would eventually mean the death of death. We should not force anyone to live indefinitely. The ethical debates concerning euthanasia that are gradually being given voice in various legal and national jurisdictions already include this as one of their themes. Yet many human beings would at least be intrigued by the idea of an extended lifetime, of a life after life, to perhaps explore the very cosmos from which all of us originate.

It is clear that life seeks none other than itself. Even after life is over, the idea of life lives on. Over a century ago, the famous historian and novelist, H.G. Wells, gave a series of lectures at the Royal Institution on the "discovery of the future." He ended his discourse in this way: "All this world is heavy with the promise of greater things, and a day will come, one day in the unending succession of days, when beings, beings who are now latent in our thoughts and hidden in our loins, shall stand upon this earth as one stands upon a footstool, and shall laugh and reach out their hands amid the stars."

Cited and Suggested Readings

Bachelard, Gaston
1958
The Poetics of Space
Beacon Press, Boston (1964)

Barthes, Roland
1971
"Change the Object Itself: Mythology Today," in *Image-Music-Text*
Noonday Press, New York. Pages 165–169 (1977)

Berger, Peter
1970
A Rumor of Angels: Modern Society and the Rediscovery of the Supernatural
Anchor Books, New York

1967
The Sacred Canopy: Elements of a Sociological Theory of Religion
Anchor Books, New York

Dewey, John
1934
Art as Experience
Perigee, Putnam. New York (1980)

Dufrenne, Mikel
1953
The Phenomenology of Aesthetic Experience
Northwestern University Press, Evanston

Durkheim, Emile
1897
Suicide
Free Press, Glencoe (1951)

Focillon, Henri
1934
The Life of Forms in Art
Zone Books, New York (1989)

Gadamer, Hans-Georg
1985
"The Experience of Death," in *The Enigma of Health*
Stanford University Press, Stanford. Pages 61–69 (1996)

1977
The Relevance of the Beautiful, and Other Essays
Cambridge University Press (1986)

Horowitz, Gregg M.
2001
Sustaining Loss: Art and Mournful Life
Stanford University Press

James, William
1907
The Varieties of Religious Experience: A Study in Human Nature
Longman's Green and Co. London (1902)

Loewen, G.V.
2008
What is God? Musings on Human Anxiety and Aspiration
AEG-Strategic Books, New York

2006
How Can We Explain the Persistence of Irrational Beliefs? Essays in Social Anthropology
The Edwin Mellen Press, Lewiston

Lukacs, Georg
1910
Soul and Form
MIT Press, Cambridge, MA

Merleau-Ponty, Maurice
1948
"The Film and the New Psychology," in *Sense and Non-Sense*
Northwestern University Press, Evanston. Pages 48–59 (1964)

1961
"Eye and Mind," in *The Primacy of Perception*
Northwestern University Press, Evanston. Pages 159–190 (1964)

1964
Signs. Northwestern University Press, Evanston.

Ricoeur, Paul
1973
"Freedom in the Light of Hope," in *The Conflict of Interpretations*
Northwestern University Press, Evanston. Pages 402–424 (1969)

Sagan, Carl
1996
The Demon-Haunted World: Science as a Candle in the Dark
Ballantyne Books, New York

Scheler, Max
2003
Ressentiment
Marquette University Press, Milwaukee (1912)

Schutz, Alfred
1967
The Phenomenology of the Social World
Northwestern University Press, Evanston (1932)

Sircello, Guy
1972
Mind and Art: an Essay on the Varieties of Expression
Princeton University Press

Wells, H.G.
1913
The Discovery of the Future
Jonathan Cape, London (1903)

Wylie, Alison, and Valerie Pinsky, eds.
1989
Critical Traditions in Contemporary Archaeology
The University of Cambridge Press, Cambridge

CPSIA information can be obtained at www.ICGtesting.com
Printed in the USA
LVOW11s1633021114

411677LV00002B/390/P